Also by Ember Grant

Magical Candle Crafting
The Book of Crystal Spells

About the Author

Ember Grant (Missouri) has been practicing the Craft for nearly twenty years. She has been contributing to *Llewellyn's Magical Almanac*, *Llewellyn's Herbal Almanac*, *Llewellyn's Spell-A-Day Almanac*, and *Llewellyn's Witches' Calendar* since 2003. Her writing has also appeared in *PanGaia*, *newWitch*, and *Circle* magazine.

To Write to the Author

If you wish to contact the author or would like more information about this book, please write to the author in care of Llewellyn Worldwide, and we will forward your request. Both the author and the publisher appreciate hearing from you and learning of your enjoyment of this book and how it has helped you. Llewellyn Worldwide cannot guarantee that every letter written to the author can be answered, but all will be forwarded. Please write to:

Ember Grant
⁒ Llewellyn Worldwide
2143 Wooddale Drive
Woodbury, MN 55125-2989

Please enclose a self-addressed stamped envelope for reply,
or $1.00 to cover costs. If outside the USA, enclose
an international postal reply coupon.

Many of Llewellyn's authors have websites with additional information and resources. For more information, please visit our website at: www.llewellyn.com.

THE SECOND
– BOOK OF –
CRYSTAL SPELLS

MORE MAGICAL USES
FOR STONES, CRYSTALS
MINERALS ... AND EVEN SALT

EMBER GRANT

Llewellyn Publications
Woodbury, Minnesota

FIRST EDITION
First Printing, 2016

Book design by Bob Gaul
Cover art by iStockphoto.com/31863690/©grafvision
              iStockphoto.com/46758584/©sorsillo
              iStockphoto.com/33981342/©Lucky_Guy
Cover design by Ellen Lawson
Editing by Rhiannon Nelson
Interior illustrations by Llewellyn Art Department

Llewellyn Publications is a registered trademark of Llewellyn Worldwide Ltd.

Library of Congress Cataloging-in-Publication Data
Names: Grant, Ember, 1971– author.
Title: The second book of crystal spells : more magical uses for stones,
    crystals, minerals, and even salt / Ember Grant.
Description: First Edition. | Woodbury : Llewellyn Worldwide, Ltd, 2016. |
    Includes bibliographical references and index. | Description based on print
    version record and CIP data provided by publisher; resource not viewed.
Identifiers: LCCN 2016005156 (print) | LCCN 2016002998 (ebook) | ISBN
    9780738748443 () | ISBN 9780738746265 (alk. paper)
Subjects: LCSH: Crystals—Miscellanea. | Precious stones—Miscellanea. |
    Occultism. | Magic.
Classification: LCC BF1442.C78 (print) | LCC BF1442.C78 G733 2016 (ebook) |
    DDC 133/.2548—dc23
LC record available at http://lccn.loc.gov/2016005156

Llewellyn Worldwide Ltd. does not participate in, endorse, or have any authority or responsibility concerning private business transactions between our authors and the public.
    All mail addressed to the author is forwarded, but the publisher cannot, unless specifically instructed by the author, give out an address or phone number.
    Any Internet references contained in this work are current at publication time, but the publisher cannot guarantee that a specific location will continue to be maintained. Please refer to the publisher's website for links to authors' websites and other sources.

Llewellyn Publications
A Division of Llewellyn Worldwide Ltd.
2143 Wooddale Drive
Woodbury, MN 55125-2989
www.llewellyn.com

Printed in the United States of America

Acknowledgments

I wish to thank all readers of *The Book of Crystal Spells*. Your interest and enthusiasm made this second book possible.

Contents

Introduction ... 1

One: The Salt of the Earth ... 3
    Types of Salt ... 5
    Specialty Salts ... 7
    Using Salt in Magic ... 8
    Salt Lamps ... 9
    Salt Spells ... 10
        Subtle Salt Protection Spell ... 11
        Protection Bundle ... 11
        Protection Bottle ... 11
        Banishing Elixir ... 12
        Salt and Fire Banishing Spell ... 12
        Salary Spell ... 13
        Crystal Water Spell ... 13
        Romantic Rose Bath ... 14
        Salt Lamp Purification Ritual ... 16
    Additional Uses ... 16

Two: Crystals and Tarot ... 19

Card and Crystal Combinations ... 20

0: The Fool ... 21

1: The Magician ... 22

2: The High Priestess ... 22

3: The Empress ... 23

4: The Emperor ... 24

5: The Hierophant (High Priest) ... 25

6: The Lovers ... 26

7: The Chariot ... 26

8: Strength ... 27

9: The Hermit ... 28

10: The Wheel of Fortune ... 29

11: Justice ... 30

12: The Hanged Man ... 31

13: Death ... 31

14: Temperance ... 32

15: The Devil ... 33

16: The Tower ... 34

17: The Star ... 35

18: The Moon ... 36

19: The Sun ... 36

20: Judgment ... 37

21: The World/Universe ... 38

Spells and Spell Techniques ... 39

Simple Spell Guidelines ... 40

Spell for Strength: A Template ... 41

Meditation to Enhance Magical Practice ... 42

The Fool: Opportunity Spell ... 42

The Chariot: Manifestation Spell ... 43

Tarot Elemental Spells and Meditations...44
    Elemental Associations...44
    Chalice Meditation—Water Element...45
    Wand Spell—Fire Element...46
    Sword Spell—Air Element...46
    Pentacle Meditation—Earth Element...46
    Fifth Element Spell...47
Court Card Correspondences...47
    Court Card Meditation...50
Decks and Readings...50
    Post-Reading Meditation...50

Three: Special Quartz Points...53
    Barnacle...54
    Bridge...55
        Bridge Quartz Connection Spell...55
    Drusy Quartz...56
        Drusy Quartz Room Spell...56
    Elestial...57
    Etched...58
    Faden...59
        Faden Quartz Seeker's Spell...59
    Fairy...60
    Fenster...60
        Fenster Quartz Window Meditation...61
    Key...61
        Key Crystal Meditation...61
    Laser Wand...62
        Laser Wand Cleansing Ritual...62
    Manifestation...63
    Phantom...64
        Phantom Crystal Dedication...65

"Reversed" Record Keeper ... 65

Scepter ... 67

    Scepter Crystal Meditation ... 67

Sheet ... 68

    Sheet Quartz Second Sight Meditation ... 68

Shovel ... 68

    Shovel Quartz Meditation ... 69

Singing ... 69

    Singing Quartz Affirmation ... 70

Spiral ... 70

    Spiral Quartz Meditation ... 71

Sprouting ... 71

    Sprouting Quartz Affirmation ... 72

Spirit ... 72

    Lift Your Spirits Meditation ... 73

Stacked ... 75

Striated ... 75

    Striated Crystal Meditation ... 76

Tabby ... 76

    Tabby Crystal Opportunity Affirmation ... 77

Trigger ... 77

    Multi-Trigger Crystals ... 78

Twin ... 79

    Twin Crystal Dedication ... 80

Aqua Aura ... 80

    Aqua Aura "Aura Cleansing" Spell ... 81

    The "I Want It All" Aqua Aura Spell ... 81

Golden Healer ... 82

Herkimer Diamond ... 83

Lavender Quartz ... 84

    Lavender Quartz Love Spell ... 84

Lithium Quartz...84
   Lithium Quartz Affirmation...85
Tangerine Quartz...85
   Tangerine Quartz Spell for Strength...86
Tibetan Quartz...86
   Tibetan Quartz Acceptance Affirmation...87

Four: Special Rock and Mineral Formations...89
Staurolite: Fairy Cross...90
   Fairy Cross Protection Amulet...90
Opal...90
   Opal "Invisibility" Spell...91
Jade...92
   Jade Spell for Decision-Making...93
Unakite...93
   Unakite Spell for Balance...94
Picasso Stone...94
   Artist's Affirmation...95
Aventurine...95
   Aventurine Opportunity Spell...95
Gypsum...96
   Gypsum Rose Motivation Spell...98
   Forgiveness Spell...98
   Selenite Past or Future Life Meditation...98
   Satin Spar Wand Spell for Focus...99
Soapstone (Steatite)...99
Anyolite (Ruby in Zoisite)...100
   Tap into Your Talents Spell...100
Septarian Nodule...101
   Acceptance Affirmation...102
Shiva Lingam Stone...102
   Shiva Lingam Dedication Ritual...103

Dalmatian Stone ... 104
  Pet Healing Spell ... 104
Hag Stones ... 105
  Hag Stone Protection Spell ... 107
  To Banish Nightmares ... 107
  Good Luck Charm ... 108
  Hag Stone Garden Spell ... 108

Five: Quartz Crystal Point Grids ... 109
Planning a Grid ... 110
  Basic Numerological Associations ... 110
  Candle Grids ... 111
  Grids for Balance and Relationships ... 111
  Maiden Mother Crone Grid ... 112
  The Pinnacle Grid ... 113
  Cross Grid ... 114
  Star Grid for Health ... 114
  Prosperity Grid ... 115
  The Feather Grid ... 116
  The Sprout Grid ... 116
  Grid for Completion ... 117
  Circles and Starbursts ... 117
More Grid Information ... 118

Six: Chalcedony Group ... 119
General Properties ... 122
Agate Spells ... 122
  Tree, Moss, and Dendritic Agates ... 122
  Ritual for Connecting with Nature ... 123
  Blue Lace Agate Affirmation ... 125
  Turritella Agate Spell to Release Worry ... 126
  Montana Agate Journey Meditation ... 127
  Crazy Lace Affirmation for Harmony ... 128

Jasper Spells...128
    Picture Jasper Spell to Uncover Fears...128
    Red Jasper Talisman for Progress...129
    Leopard Jasper Endurance Spell...129
Other Types of Chalcedony...130
    Carnelian Energy Spell...130
    Bloodstone Talisman for Courage...131
    Chrysoprase: Adaptability Affirmation...132

Seven: Sixth Sense: Stones for Enhancing Intuition...135
Amethyst...137
Chevron Amethyst...138
Seer Stone...139
Lavender Quartz...140
Black Sapphire...140
Herkimer Diamond...141
Purple Fluorite...142
Lapis Lazuli...143
Apophyllite...143
Azurite...144
    Journey Meditation: Spirit Realm...144
Iolite...145
Kyanite...146
Kunzite...147
General Intuition Spell...148

Eight: Crystal Rituals and Spells for Sabbats and Esbats...149
Imbolc...150
    Crystal Altar for Imbolc...150
    Imbolc Ritual for a Group...152
Ostara: Spring Equinox...154
    Crystal Altar for Ostara...155
    Ostara/Storm Moon Healing Ritual for a Group...156

Beltane...159
   Abundance Spell...159
   Beltane Passion Amulet...160
Midsummer: Summer Solstice...161
   Crystal Spell for Midsummer...162
   Fire Purging Ritual...163
Lughnasadh: First Harvest...165
   Skill Enhancement Spell...166
   Lughnasadh Group Ritual...166
Autumn Equinox: Harvest...169
   Crystal Cornucopia...169
Samhain: New Year...170
   Samhain Divination Spell...171
   Group Ritual for Samhain...172
Yule: Winter Solstice—The Return of the Sun...174
   Ritual to Welcome the Sun...175
   Fire and Ice: Winter Solstice Group Ritual...175
Other Ritual Ideas...176
   Elemental Stones...176
   Quarter Call...177
   Evocation...177
Moon Rituals...178
   New Moon Ritual for Renewal...178
   Dark Moon Journey Meditation...180
   Full Moon Ritual...181

Conclusion: Pay Attention...183

Appendix...185

Stones and Metals: Metaphysical Correspondences...185

Crystal Systems...203

Platonic Solids...208

Planetary Associations...211

Correspondences for Days of the Week:
    Stones, Incense, and Oils...211

Chakra Stones...213

Seasonal Associations...215

Stones by Use...215

Colors...220

Geometric Shapes...222

Glossary...223

Bibliography...229

Index...237

Introduction

My previous book on crystals grew from my love of collecting and working with stones, and was based on the pieces in my collection. Naturally, like all collectors, I am constantly adding new pieces and finding new ways to use them. There was no way to fit everything I wanted to share in that first book, and I have acquired more pieces since then as well. So, the only logical thing to do was to begin a second book.

This book contains new material but may refer to and build upon skills mentioned in *The Book of Crystal Spells*. I have listened to reviewers and interviewers, as well as those who contacted me online, and have tried to include areas of interest that were requested. However, if a piece you love is missing, please accept my apologies. There's only so much room in a book, and I don't own every mineral (unfortunately!). Some chapters are sorted by style—for example, grids and tarot; others are grouped by type of stone—quartz points and chalcedony. There's a chapter for sabbat and esbat rituals, and a chapter on stones specifically for enhancing your sixth sense. The first chapter is an in-depth exploration of using salt in magic, and you'll also find a chapter that contains an interesting assortment of special rock and mineral formations. You can read the chapters in order or jump around. The appendix has been expanded in this book, with more than twenty new stones. And, just as before, I've included them because they're stones with which I have hands-on experience.

This book was written mainly with Wiccan practitioners in mind, as well as anyone interested in folk magic, modern Witchcraft, or even Western ceremonial magic. As it is assumed the reader already has a basic knowledge of one or more of these areas, specific directions for preparation of ritual space, circle casting, and so on, are not included.

In addition, since methods of cleansing, charging, and dedicating stones were explored in the previous book, those subjects are not addressed here. I believe a good sequel builds upon its predecessor and takes the reader into new territory. As with the previous book, I'd like to point out this is not a book of crystal healing, but there are some spells for generating healing energy. Crystal magic and crystal healing are different practices, but there is some overlap.

Just as before, I have included rhyming chants with most of the spells and meditations. From my perspective, this helps with visualization and affirming one's intent. Rhymes and rhythm make chants easier to remember and repeat. However, feel free to write personal statements instead or simply remain silent—make these spells your own. No matter which type of magic you practice, remember to focus your attention and avoid your rituals and spells becoming simply recitation of words. Visualization and intent are vital to your success—the power is inside you. Just saying words or performing an action is not enough.

Thank you, readers, for joining me in the love of crystals.

Happy spellcasting!

– ONE –

THE SALT OF THE EARTH

Several years ago, I received a Himalayan salt lamp as a gift. At first I thought it was a giant chunk of rose quartz—it was a lovely shade of salmon-pink, carved to hold a tea light candle. Naturally, I became intrigued by this "new" pink salt and began a journey of exploration. I was unaware of the immense variety of salts and became delighted by their beautiful colors and subtle differences in taste. I began collecting different types of salt from around the world, experimenting with them in the kitchen, and thought: why not add this variety of salt to my magical practice?

Salt is celebrating a rise in popularity—the presence of trace minerals that give salts different colors makes these salts more sought-after and, consequently, more expensive.

The various colors are the result of "impurities" or other minerals present in the salt. Many people favor this because it means the salt contains a spectrum of trace minerals not found in refined salts—some people believe, when it comes to salt, "pure" and "refined" are not necessarily good things.

Compare it to white bread versus whole grain. The white may be pretty, but it lacks the nutrients of whole wheat. Of course, critics say it's silly to pay more for what is essentially just "dirty" salt. I'll let you decide.

So why include salt in a book on crystal magic? First of all, salt is a crystal. And it's the only mineral humans eat in its pure form. Halite, rock salt, is the mineral form of sodium chloride. It occurs naturally in the water of our oceans, in shallow areas called marshes, and it is also mined from underground places that have formed as the result of ancient seas that have dried up. Halite is the most common of the halide group—a group that contains 150 minerals.

The familiar phrases "worth his salt" and "earning his salt" further illustrate just how vital salt has been throughout history. The mineral Homer referred to as divine, and that Plato declared to be held particularly in high regard by the gods, all over the world throughout all of recorded history, salt has been revered, coveted, and highly valued. It's one of the most ancient minerals used by humans; prehistoric people used it to preserve meats, since it prevents dehydration. It was also used for healing—the chlorine present in salt kills bacteria. To remove bitterness from their greens, the Romans salted them. This is where we get the word *salad* (salted).

One of the names given to the people we call Celts (which came from the Greek *Keltoi*) is the Gauls or Galli. The Romans called them this, and it comes from another Greek word, used by the Egyptians—*hal*, meaning salt. This is because so many places associated with salt were used by the Celtic people. While we acknowledge there is much mystery about these people, we know for certain they extensively mined and traded salt and salted meats (for which they appear to have been especially known).

Salt has a fascinating history; its impact cannot be overstated. Folklore surrounding salt is rich with examples from all around the world. Many cultures associate the giving of salt, along with bread, as a welcome gift for a new home. Ancient cultures, including the Greeks, Romans, and Egyptians, used salt in sacred offerings and to invoke the gods. In fact, according to the book *Salt: A World History*, salt water is said to be the "the origin of Christian holy water."

Types of Salt

You may be wondering about the difference between rock salt and sea salt. Sea salt comes from evaporated sea water; rock salt comes from underground mines. Other than that, they aren't much different. Chemically, they are both still sodium chloride.

Rock salt is usually a grayish color, but impurities (other minerals) can cause different shades. Unrefined salt is usually not pure white—it can be gray, pink, or even blue. More than 90 different minerals can be found in unrefined salt. Table salt is basically just refined rock salt; the large grains are broken down into tiny ones and iodine is often added to provide people with this essential nutrient. Sometimes iron is also added to salt.

Sea salts are often considered a better choice for cooking than table salt due to their milder flavor. Sea salts are often used in spa treatments; many people enjoy the rejuvenating power of salt while bathing—it can help with circulation, sore muscles, and is even used to cleanse the body of impurities. You don't have to buy or make fancy bath salts (but you certainly can!), you can just add some salt to your bath. Epsom salt is not actually salt, so it's not included here. But it is a valuable mineral compound of magnesium and sulfate that is also essential for a soothing bath and has many other practical uses.

Sea salt is obtained from evaporation ponds or ancient deposits. The sea does not actually "collect" salt, but salt forms in the water because of the presence of a variety of dissolved minerals. Even rock salt comes from the sea, from places where old seas evaporated and were buried. So, technically, all salt is "sea" salt.

Kosher salt grains are smaller than sea salt but larger than standard table salt. This salt is called "kosher" because it's used in the koshering process; for meat to be certified as kosher, salt is used to draw out the blood. This type of salt is used because the grains have a flattened shape, allowing them to dissolve more slowly and remain on the meat longer. This salt can be derived from sea salt or rock salt.

Here's a brief summary of the main types of salt:

- *Rock salt:* Mined from the ground instead of being evaporated. In its unrefined state it's used mainly for industrial purposes.

- *Table salt (iodized):* The most common salt, table salt is highly refined rock salt with anti-caking agents added to prevent clumping. Harvested from mines. Iodine has been added since the 1920s to prevent iodine deficiency.

- *Sea salt:* Salt created by evaporating sea water (as opposed to being mined from the ground). Very flavorful due to the presence of many trace minerals.

- *Kosher salt:* A special shape of salt grains used to preserve meats. Commonly used in cooking.

- *Pickling salt:* Lacks the anti-caking agents used in table salt to avoid the brine becoming cloudy as the salt dissolves. Sometimes referred to as canning salt.

- *Finishing salt:* Unique cooking salts often made by hand in small batches; sometimes used as a garnish.

- *Flake salt:* Evaporated sea water is slowly heated to produce interesting delicate crystal shapes.

- *Smoked salts:* As the name indicates, these salts are smoked, sometimes with other flavors added. Look for naturally smoked salts, not salt that has been artificially flavored with liquid smoke.

- *Flavored salts:* Salts that are infused with flavors of herbs, spices, and other extracts.

Specialty Salts

Gourmet salts are one of the hottest foodie trends. While some of these salts can be expensive, you should be able to buy small quantities for a reasonable price either online or at a spice shop. Many places sell sampler assortments. There are many more than I've listed here; these are the ones I've been using that are easy to find and relatively inexpensive.

Some of the salts in this list are naturally occurring salts with trace minerals that give them special color; others have been created by adding extracts or have been infused with flavors. Also, remember you can often choose between fine or coarse grain when purchasing. I like to buy coarse grains and keep a grinder or salt mill on hand if I want to create a smaller size. There are simply too many for the scope of this book, but if you're intrigued by these salts, have fun exploring!

- *Gray Sea Salt (sel gris)* is sometimes called Celtic Gray or French Gray. The soft gray color is derived from the clay in the salt water beds; it's hand-harvested with wooden tools. Fleur de Sel is a special French salt—"flower of salt"—harvested from small ponds by hand in a similar tradition, but these are only the surface crystals. Only harvested between May and September. Often used as a finishing salt. There is also a Portuguese version of this salt, flor de sal.

- *Himalayan Pink:* The lovely color of this salt is caused by the presence of minerals in the specific location. Mined along the coast of the Himalayan Mountains and inland Peru, this salt is prized for its delicate flavor and unique color. There are other varieties of pink salt from other locations.

- *Persian Blue:* From Iran; intense pressure on the crystals causes some of the salt grains to display a blue color—an optical illusion due to the fracturing of light, not the presence of trace minerals.

- *Black Lava:* A Hawaiian sea salt blended with activated charcoal. The color is merely decorative. The charcoal is usually derived from burned coconut shells. Often used as a finishing salt in cooking.

- *Hawaiian Alaea:* A reddish-colored salt due to iron oxide from the volcanic clay in the region. It was once used only for rituals and religious feasts. Mainly used in cooking as a finishing salt.

- *Bamboo Jade:* A lovely green-colored salt from Hawaii; the color is due to the addition of bamboo leaf extract.

Using Salt in Magic

Metaphysically, the origins of salt in magic make sense—it's a preservative. It cleanses and protects. So why use different salts? For the same reason we use them in cooking—flavor. Like other stones, these minerals have different personalities. They can add variety to your magical practice.

I have been using these salts in my practice, along with a smoked salt flavored with bourbon (yes, it tastes as good as it sounds). When you buy some special salt, consider dividing the package to save some for your kitchen. This way you can also experiment with cooking, using these salts by adding them to your kitchen witchery.

To begin experimenting, consider color. For example, since black has long been considered a protective color, use black salts for protection, banishing, or binding. Red is a color often used for protection as well, but it can also be used for passion; pink can be used for love. Or, consider the presence of the other minerals as making the salt more grounding—the presence of clay, for example, in gray or red salts. You can even consider the region from which the salt was obtained, if applicable.

If spending extra money for special salts is too inconvenient or you have trouble finding them, start with just one. The pink Himalayan variety is very popular in most grocery stores and is probably the most affordable. Additionally, limit your use of colored salt to special occasions or mix it with table or sea salt.

Of course, if you can't find any of these special salts you can still experiment with expanding your use of salt in magic. If you've been using table salt, try sea salt. As with anything from nature, we want it as minimally processed as possible for magical use—the less refined the product, the better. Since larger grains are often easier to work with, rock salt, sea salt, and kosher salt are all good, affordable choices. Table salt is still perfectly acceptable to use, especially if you require large amounts to fill a spell bottle or create a large shape or grid.

Store salts for magic just as you would in your kitchen, in glass jars or zipper bags with a tight seal; avoid exposure to water or high humidity.

Salt Lamps

Salt lamps have grown in popularity just as the specialty salts for cooking. As I mentioned earlier, these gorgeous salt "lamps" are large chunks of pink Himalayan salt with a hole carved inside for a candle, or they're made to hold a light bulb and be electrically powered. I have both styles and each type has its strengths; the rosy glow of light is very tranquil for magical or mundane use. This salt is from ancient deposits that are mainly located in Pakistan. If you have difficulty thinking of salt as a crystal, these lamps will change your mind.

The reason for their popularity is, like the salt for cooking, this type of salt contains natural minerals that are lacking in refined salt. The presence of iron oxide creates the pink color. Enthusiasts like these lamps for their health claims of purifying the air. While this has not been scientifically proven, metaphysically salt is used to purify and repel negativity, so they are ideal for purification spells. These salt lamps are beautiful and natural, an asset to any room or altar, and another way to take advantage of crystal magic. Additionally, you may find these lamps made from white salt as well. Since halite has a cubic structure, which we associate with the most grounding and "earthy" of minerals, you can use these lamps to create a soothing atmosphere and connect with the earth element.

Remember to clean your lamp carefully—water dissolves salt! Dust it gently with a dry (or only slightly damp) cloth.

Salt Spells

While each spell here calls for a specific type and color of salt, remember you can substitute regular table salt, kosher salt, or general sea salt at any time.

Salt appears in folklore from many cultures as a protective charm. In Europe in the Middle Ages, farmers used brine (salty water) to save grain from fungal infections. Some even used salt to bless their plows. Since salt has a reputation for protection, it naturally came to be used for all manner of guarding against evil spirits, or just spirits in general. From Japanese, Haitian, African, and Caribbean traditions, there are stories of salt being used for these purposes. In some instances, even handling salt was considered dangerous because it was such a potent charm. A sixteenth-century book of Jewish law stated that salt should only be touched with the middle two fingers; in Medieval Europe, salt was only touched with a knife tip at the table—never with the hands.

There are many approaches you can take for these spells. A bottle is ideal for protecting a home, or you can use bits of salt in the corners of individual rooms. You can carry a bundle of salt with you as well.

Subtle Salt Protection Spell

This is perfect for places where you don't want the salt to be noticed. A tiny pinch or a few small grains will go unnoticed in a corner. Use black, red, or white salt, and perform this spell on a waning moon day or during a dark moon phase. As you place the grains in each corner, visualize the room being cleansed and chant:

Salt dispel; all be well.

Protection Bundle

Use coarse grains of red or white salt; wrap in a bundle or drawstring bag of red or white cloth. You can also add herbs, if you like—a crumbled bay leaf is an ideal choice. Carry the bundle with you.

Protection Bottle

Choose a small bottle or jar you can seal with a cap, cork, or lid and gather black, red, and white salts. If you don't have these specific colors, just use what you have on hand. Charge the salts in the sun for a few hours prior to adding them to the bottle. Create the bottle on a full moon day, or when the moon is waxing. Layer the salts in the bottle—it's okay if they blend together. You can also add a small, clear quartz point, if you wish. Once you have filled the bottle, seal the spell with these words:

Guard this home, safe and sound, by this salt, the spell is bound.

Visualize your home, and all within, being protected. Store the bottle in the home near the main entrance or threshold area, or near a window.

Hint: To keep the layers of salt from running together (creating an attractive layered effect), put the smallest grains on the bottom and increase the size toward the top (otherwise small grains will simply sink down between the coarser grains). If you don't have enough salt to fill the bottle, use a combination of salt and sand.

Banishing Elixir

Use Black Lava Salt for this spell—simply dissolve your desired amount of salt in water and transfer it to a jar or spray bottle. The black color will darken the water as the salt dissolves. This makes a nice room spray, or you can sprinkle it as needed.

On a waning or dark moon night, place the salt in the water. If you can, let the mixture sit overnight (unless you're in a hurry). Stir the water around in a counterclockwise motion from time to time, visualizing the banishment of negative energy. After you have poured the mixture into a container for storage (or for immediate use), hold your projective hand over the bottle, continuing your visualization, and chant:

> *Salt and water, cleanse this place,*
> *banish ill without a trace.*

Salt and Fire Banishing Spell

This is a more intense banishing spell than the elixir—this one uses the fire element. The projective, transforming energy of fire can help you quickly banish something in your way. While the Banishing Elixir is best used for general dispelling of negativity, this Banishing Spell can be used for something more specific.

This spell is best done outdoors with a large fire—a campfire, bonfire, or a patio fire pit. Use Black Lava Salt, if you have it. Place a bit of salt in your palm as you visualize what you wish to banish. Using coarse salt makes it easier to handle. Pinch it between your fingertips, continuing to visualize, and throw it—not a gentle toss—into the fire while shouting "Be gone!" Name what you are banishing. Be forceful.

Salary Spell

Salt, like other spices throughout history, once served as a form of monetary exchange. The Romans paid soldiers with rations of salt; they called this *salarium*, the origin of our word "salary." In addition, the Latin word *sal* became the French world *solde* (meaning "pay") which became the word *soldier*. The use of salt as currency makes salt a good choice for prosperity spells.

For this spell, use coarse, green-colored Bamboo Jade Salt, if possible. Not only is the green color appropriate, but bamboo extract, which causes the color, is also associated with good luck (as well as protection). Find a green or white drawstring bag or use a piece of green cloth you can tie with a ribbon. You will also need a coin of your choice and a dried basil leaf. Place three teaspoons of the salt, the basil, and the coin into the bag. Visualize your goal and chant:

I am worth my salt, I know, let abundance grow and grow.

Carry the bundle with you or keep it on your altar.

Crystal Water Spell

Our bodies need salt (yet it is possible to consume too much). Salt is beneficial for the body inside and out and there are many health remedies using salt. If you've ever gargled with salt water to soothe a sore throat, you know how well it works. Salt water rinses can help with sore gums and toothaches, too. Many people even use a saline rinse for their sinuses. *Disclaimer:* Home remedies should not replace seeking professional help; always consult a physician.

One technique is to make sole water (pronounced "so-lay"; named for the sun)—not to be confused with the Sole brand name of Italian mineral water. This is a saltwater elixir that many people claim has health benefits. This practice involves making a solution of water and sea salt in which the water absorbs so much salt that no more salt will dissolve in it. Half a teaspoon of this salt water is added to drinking water each morning. Research this carefully if you plan to try it. You can find recipes online (see bibliography).

The sole method is the inspiration for this spell, which only uses one small grain of sea salt. You will dissolve the salt crystal in an 8-ounce glass of warm water and drink it.

Since blue is a color often associated with comfort and healing, select one coarse grain of Persian Blue Sea Salt—find one with striking blue accents. Additionally, the elements of earth and water are often used for healing magic and this spell, using a crystal and water, combines both. Water and earth are nurturing and receptive. And halite has a cubic structure, associated with earth.

This spell is a way to visualize healing energy. If you wish to focus on removing something, visualize it dissolving as the salt dissolves, and perform this spell during a waning moon phase. Otherwise, use the waxing or full moon phase to increase good health.

As the salt dissolves, visualize the earth and water elements combining. Focus on optimum good health, vitality, and healing energy. As you drink, take these elements into your body, continuing to visualize any healing you need or just general good health. Remember, you're actually drinking a dissolved crystal!

Romantic Rose Bath

One of the folklore beliefs associated with salt is fertility. This may seem counterintuitive, since we know nothing will grow in salted soil. But ancient civilizations noticed that salt was associated with the sea and the abundance of fish. The Romans had a word for a man being in love—*salax*, "in a salted state." This is where our word "salacious" comes from. Brides and grooms from France and Germany in ancient lore carried salt on their wedding day; Egyptian priests abstained from salt because they considered it a threat to their celibacy, since it increased desire.

You will create a very small batch of bath salts for this spell. Bath salts may be an obvious use of salt in magic, but let's face it—a chapter on salt magic needs at least one bath salt spell! This version is a delightful combination of pink Himalayan sea salt, rose oil, and dried rose petals. You can also use it for a soothing foot soak. You can make a larger batch of these salts if you wish, but since rose oil is costly, I usually just make enough for a couple uses.

You will need:

- One handful of coarse pink sea salt
- Several drops of rose oil (essential or fragrance)
- Six dried rose petals, pink or red
- Mix all ingredients and use immediately or store in an air-tight jar or plastic zipper bag.

This spell is for any romantic situation. You can use it when preparing for a special evening, sharing the bath with a partner, or to increase self-love and pamper yourself. As you mix the ingredients, visualize loving thoughts and whatever specific goal you may have.

Like the Crystal Water Spell, this, too, incorporates the elements of earth and water—both receptive and nurturing. Prepare the room by lighting candles and creating a peaceful atmosphere. If you dislike bits of herbs floating in your bath water, make a sachet for your bath salts using a mesh drawstring bag instead of just tossing them in the water. The salt will dissolve and the essential oils will disperse into the water but the herbs won't.

You can dry out the bag, discard the herbs (or reuse them), and refill the bag, using it over and over. For showers, let water run over the drawstring bag of bath salts before splashing it onto your body. Or, dissolve the bag of salts in warm water and anoint yourself with the water before, during, or after showering.

In general, you can create just about any combination of bath salts in this manner, using whatever essential oil(s) and dried herbs or flowers you wish.

Salt Lamp Purification Ritual

Light your salt lamp and stand before it—this can be done with an electric lamp as well as a candle holder. Visualize the light penetrating the salt and filling the room with pure, magical light. If you wish, make a circle of clear quartz points around your lamp, facing outward. Chant the word *mundaret* three times.

Mundaret is Latin for "purify" or "cleanse." Sometimes I like to use Latin for chants because it gives a more formal atmosphere to the spell. You can just say "purify" or "cleanse" if you wish.

Additional Uses

Here's a summary and some additional ways to use salt in your magical practice:

- Choose specialty salts based on color associations or regional associations.
- Mix salt with sand to use as the border for a magic circle or for grids. To form lines (or fill bottles) with salt, roll a piece of paper into a cone or use a funnel.
- For protection from negative energy, put a pinch of salt in the corners of rooms, thresholds, or the bedroom (to prevent nightmares).

- Create salt and stone mixtures to carry in pouches or display in bowls.

- Throw salt into fire or water.

- Purify yourself with a saltwater bath prior to a ritual or spell. Quick Sink Purification: Prior to spell work, rituals, etc., you can quickly wash your hands with a purifying salt elixir in your bathroom sink. Plug the drain, sprinkle salt in the basin, and add water. Simple!

- Make a salt elixir to cleanse tools or other objects.

- Place stones on a bed of salt to cleanse.

- Create spell jars or bottles using salt or a mixture of sand, salt, herbs, and stones.

- You can make a non-edible black salt for magical use by adding fireplace ash to ordinary salt. Alternately, you can use scrapings from an iron skillet or cauldron.

Imagine the world when spices were traded as currency—spices that we have today casually stored in jars in our cupboards, or the salt we pour on the streets to melt snow. We take them for granted, often forgetting that some of them were worth their weight (or more) in gold. When you use salt for magical purposes, remember its long history and value.

– TWO –

CRYSTALS AND TAROT

I love working with the tarot, so combining the cards with crystals has been a delightful project for me. I spent weeks combing through all my various decks and resources, compiling general key words and investigating the stones that seemed to best resonate with each card.

You probably already know that using crystals to purify and protect a tarot deck is a common practice. You can also hold stones during readings or place them on the table near the cards. There are some exercises, meditations, and spells in this chapter that are more specific; they are connected to an individual card and allow you to access the potential and qualities each one possesses. You can combine stones and tarot cards in grids and layouts, as well as using them for visualization and meditation. Often a card you receive in a reading, or one you draw for the day, has a special significance—crystals can help you manifest that influence or give you insight into something you need to know.

Card and Crystal Combinations

For each card I have listed some key words—this is not intended to replace an in-depth study of the tarot. However, those who do study and use the tarot will be able to add their own insight to this process. If you're new to tarot, using key words is a good way to introduce yourself to the various interpretations and characteristics of each card.

The stones listed come from my research and subtle ways the stone matches the "personality" of the card. There are several stones to choose from for each card, allowing you to narrow the focus of your intention. See the appendix for detailed descriptions of each stone.

After the list of stones for each card, you will find some questions for exploring the qualities of the card. These are intended to guide your spell work. For example, if you receive a particular card in a reading, you can use these questions to explore what that card's appearance means for you, then choose a stone (or stones) that corresponds to that card, and meditate on that meaning. Alternately, select an area you wish to work on, choose that card and a corresponding stone, and meditate on developing those skills. I have also listed each card's possible uses in magic. Techniques for spells are provided at the end of the chapter, along with some specific spells and meditations.

The brief card descriptions offered here are general and are not full-fledged divinatory meanings; rather, they are descriptive of the experience each card represents on the Fool's journey through the Major Arcana—often described as the journey of the soul through life's challenges. The key words and symbols used here are based on the Rider-Waite deck, but they have been cross-referenced with at least two other decks to include a wide range of possibilities. Reversed meanings are not explored here.

Remember: While the stones I've listed are my personal interpretations, don't discount your existing associations and your instinct. If my selections don't feel right to you, explore and find those that resonate with your personal experience. And, naturally, there may be some over-lap. The characteristics of some of the cards have commonalities, as do many of the stones.

You may want to designate a deck to use specifically for spells—that way any residual energy the cards pick up will not affect your readings. Plus, as with crystal dedication, repeated use of an item for the same purpose reinforces its power.

0: *The Fool*

Most tarot resources describe this card as the beginning of a journey—the journey of the soul through the stages represented in the Major Arcana, a journey of development that contains the entirety of the human experience.

Key words: innocence, risk-taking, impulse, inner child, enthusiasm, adventure, a quest—also foolishness and carelessness or extravagance

- Bornite (also called "Peacock Ore")
- Herkimer Diamond
- Pearl
- Soapstone
- Zircon

Ask Yourself: Where are you going in life? What fun, exciting, and new experiences would you like to have? Do you let faith and trust guide you? The possibilities are wide open at this time.

Magical Uses: To lighten up and learn to be present in the moment, free from worry about the past or the future. To open the way for new opportunities and possibilities.

1: The Magician

This card represents the spark of something new—creation, training, the development of skill and power; the Magician stands for the power of life itself.

Key Words: the mind, beginnings, willpower, goals, creativity, skill, personal power, individuality, self-control, confidence, and imagination

- Aventurine
- Hematite
- Howlite
- Moonstone
- Tiger Eye
- Wulfenite
- Yellow Fluorite

Ask Yourself: Do I have clear objectives and a focus for my energy? How do I communicate and express myself? Are there skills I need to learn or perfect? Do I have a strong sense of self?

Magical Uses: Use with your personal power stone (see *The Book of Crystal Spells*); to enhance focus, attention, and magical skills; to enhance intellectual ability.

2: The High Priestess

If the Magician can be said to represent a masculine figure, the High Priestess can be seen as a feminine archetype of power. Often associated with the Moon Goddesses of many cultures, she guards many secrets, mysteries, and wisdom about life. This card can also symbolize the subconscious mind—our inner wisdom. At this early stage of the journey, this card represents that there are great truths and life lessons to be learned.

Key Words: intuition, knowledge, mystery, awareness, the subconscious mind, peace, serenity, psychic abilities, wisdom, perception, initiation (and science)

- Lapis Lazuli
- Moonstone
- Opal

Ask Yourself: Am I seeking knowledge? What aspects of myself do I need to discover? Am I developing my insight? Do my dreams seem to be telling me something? Seek the knowledge within.

Magical Uses: guidance, enhance psychic ability, protection, wisdom, dream magic (use Celestite), divination, clairvoyance

3: The Empress

This card is often seen as the Great Mother archetype. If we consider her presence at this phase of the journey, she represents the primitive life force—nourishment and sensory experience.

Key Words: fertility, abundance, nurturing, warmth, prosperity, passion, wealth, luck, pleasure, nourishment, creativity, nature, home, maternal instincts, loyalty

- Carnelian
- Diamond
- Emerald
- Garnet
- Geode
- Gypsum
- Jasper
- Picasso Stone

- Rose Quartz
- Sapphire
- Tiger Eye

Ask Yourself: What creative projects need my attention? Am I developing/
using the nurturing aspects of the Mother figure? Do I feel inspired
and nurtured? Do I explore the senses and enjoy pleasure? Fertility
is not just reproduction—it's creating things, growing.

Magical Uses: wealth, abundance, fertility, conception, creativity,
passion, good fortune, healing

4: *The Emperor*

Often considered a disciplinary figure, the Emperor has a reputation for
appearing as a stern, authoritarian ruler. We meet this character next on
our journey to remind us that yes, we need the pleasure the Empress gives
us, but we also need rules and order in our lives. We may not always like
the rules, but they are necessary to avoid chaos. And, we must learn to
follow these rules as we mature. The Emperor can be said to symbolize
civilization. Think of him as a father figure.

Key Words: order, rules, power, reason, boundaries, strength, planning
for long-range goals, discipline, authority, father figure, protection,
leadership, courage, vitality, confidence

- Aragonite
- Bronzite
- Fluorite (clear or blue)
- Iron
- Onyx
- Pyrite

- Sodalite
- Zebra Rock

Ask Yourself: Am I organized and disciplined in my pursuits? What are my ambitions and goals? What type of leadership skills do I have or need to develop? How do I respond to authority? You can achieve whatever you set your mind on. Be ambitious.

Magical Uses: starting projects, building self-confidence, pursuit of a goal, strength, protection, discipline, patience, endurance, assertiveness

5: The Hierophant (High Priest)

Try not to think of this card as representing religious dogma; think instead of morality and values. The Emperor gives us laws, rules, and responsibility; the High Priest extends that with the moral codes we live by. Rooted in intelligence and knowledge, these are the social institutions and what they represent to a culture.

Key Words: social conventions, teaching, traditions, spiritual knowledge, revelation, compassion, kindness, and mercy

- Amethyst
- Apatite
- Bronzite

Ask Yourself: What are my morals and values? Do I live by them? Do I need guidance or training of some kind? Where will I find it? What traditions do I follow? Do I fight boundaries or break them—and what effect does this have on myself and others? What do I need to learn? What can I teach or give to others? Get in touch with your higher self and your inner guide.

Magical Uses: teaching, public speaking

6: The Lovers

The Lovers card represents relationships, but sometimes it stands for choice. At this stage of the journey through the Major Arcana, the soul is maturing and preparing for separation from parents—moving on to an adult life. This card can also symbolize adolescence and discovery of one's own beliefs, desires, and ideals.

Key Words: relationships, choice, fulfillment, beauty, commitment, sex, love, attraction, union, equality between male and female—also being tested

- Azurite
- Morganite
- Peridot
- Rhodocrosite
- Rhodonite
- Rose Quartz
- Unakite

Ask Yourself: What relationships do I have with others? Are those relationships satisfying? If not, why? Are there decisions that need to be made—am I avoiding them? Am I clinging to old ways of thought or the ideals of others? Am I being true to myself and what I need/want? Be yourself. Knowing yourself (and acknowledging that) will help bring honesty and peace to all your personal relationships.

Magical Uses: relationships, balance, choices, decision-making

7: The Chariot

This card represents accomplishment—the soul has reached adulthood. Everything that has been learned on the journey culminates here. And yet, there can be contradictions. The will of the individual is focused, energy applied to a goal, but we must not let our accomplishments represent who we are. We are more than our tasks and successes. We know our purpose, but we can't let it define who we are.

Key Words: will and purpose, overcoming obstacles, belief in solutions, success, victory, conquest, triumph, and ambition

- Agate
- Barite Rose
- Citrine
- Hemimorphite
- Labradorite
- Sulfur
- Turquoise

Ask Yourself: What face do I show to the world—is it authentic? Is it the real me? If not, why? What am I hiding, or hiding from? Am I making progress toward my goal without letting it consume me? Do I let my deeds or my occupation define who I am? What victories do I seek? Do I feel out of control? Free yourself from defining who you are by what you do or your relationships; celebrate your successes.

Magical Uses: confidence, finding one's purpose, victory

8: Strength

Outward success has been achieved; maturity has been reached. Now it's time to look within. Much of the journey of cards 1–7 concerns outward experiences—society, learning, growing up, relationships. The journey now takes an inward turn. There is a subtle feminine quality to this card; the strength displayed here is not one of physical power but more of persuasion, gentleness, and trust. It takes real strength to look within, to find inner strength, to discover who we really are.

Key Words: confidence, self-discovery, emotional and mental strength, determination, restraint

- Hemimorphite
- Rutilated Quartz
- Tiger Eye
- Sodalite
- Smoky Quartz

Ask Yourself: What I am passionate about? Am I following my passion? Do I feel strong and courageous enough to pursue my dreams? Do I have the courage to take risks? Do I have a harmonious balance of emotional and physical love in my life? Do I love without judgment? Strength is not always physical. We need emotional strength as well.

Magical Uses: strength for physical body and/or emotions, desire, courage, creativity

9: The Hermit

The journey within continues. Hermits often withdraw from society to pursue some kind of individual quest—usually for knowledge or spirituality. This character looks within to learn more about himself and the world. In darkness, they find light. This character can be seen as a guide, sharing what he or she learns. Spending time alone, contemplating life and seeking knowledge, the Hermit grows in many ways. The soul continues to mature.

Key Words: study and analysis, looking inward, meditation, solitude, soul-searching, enlightenment, spiritual inspiration, reflection

- Ametrine
- Calcite

- Fluorite (clear)
- Lodestone
- Picasso Stone
- Serpentine
- Rutilated Quartz
- Tibetan Quartz
- Vanadinite

Ask Yourself: Do I use my time wisely? Do I feel enlightened? What do I seek? What knowledge or experience is missing from my life? Do I meditate regularly? Let your higher self guide you.

Magical Uses: vision quests, spiritual journeys, patience, study, meditation

10: *The Wheel of Fortune*

Like games of chance, many things in life are out of our control. The Wheel turns, bringing fortune as well as misfortune. The only thing we can control is our reaction to what life brings. Additionally, this card represents a kind of rebirth, the turning of the wheel of life.

Key Words: success, good fortune, rebirth, acceptance, destiny, fate, consequences, culmination, conclusion

- Aventurine
- Chiastolite
- Dolomite
- Quartz with Black Tourmaline
- Rhyolite

Ask Yourself: How do I adapt when faced with change? Are there issues in my life that need to be resolved? Do I feel out of control when faced with unexpected challenges? Meet new experiences with the attitude that you will grow and learn from them.

Magical Uses: to induce a change, luck in gambling, expansion of opportunity, acceptance of change

11: Justice

We're still on the inward journey—this time, Justice asks us to take an honest look at ourselves and our lives. The symbol of the scales demands that we seek balance in a variety of ways. This can be very challenging.

Key Words: balance, honesty, self-assessment and self-reflection, cause and effect, integrity, equilibrium, equality, fairness, honor, poise, virtue, harmony

- Amazonite
- Apophyllite
- Bloodstone
- Desert Rose (crystallized gypsum)
- Granite
- Hemimorphite
- Mica
- Onyx
- Rhyolite
- Snowflake Obsidian

Ask Yourself: How do I respond when I need to make a decision? Do I feel balanced? Am I being honest with myself? Do I recognize my strengths and weaknesses? Go deep and get in touch with the "darkness"—the unacknowledged parts of yourself.

Magical Uses: legal matters, truth, clarity of thought, self-reflection

12: *The Hanged Man*

Some see this card as the Fool being stuck—hung up—on some problem or challenge. Others say this card represents self-sacrifice and change. These two interpretations can go hand in hand. Getting stuck can be a catalyst for change; these situations can also require some kind of personal sacrifice that is necessary to move forward. This character can also represent someone who is comfortable in his own skin—this kind of confidence prepares the Fool for the next stage of the inward journey.

Key Words: sacrifice, wisdom, transformation, transition, change, inner peace, new perspective

- Black Sapphire
- Lepidolite
- Malachite
- Peridot
- Soapstone (Steatite)
- Topaz

Ask Yourself: Are there sacrifices I need to make in my life? How do I feel about sacrifices I have made? What am I avoiding? Do I feel trapped or stagnant? Achievement often requires sacrifice for greater gains.

Magical Uses: mystical visions, altered states, to end stagnation, surrender

13: *Death*

If the Justice card represents self-understanding, and the Hanged Man stands for trusting the process of change, the Death card symbolizes a third part of this transitional experience—letting go of part of ourselves we no longer need. This card is often the source of fear and anxiety when it appears in readings, but it does not mean physical death. It's interesting to note that the French phrase *la petite mort* is sometimes used to refer to an orgasm as the "little death," as particularly a state of weakness or change in consciousness. Another type of release of the self is found here.

Key Words: change, transformation/transition, alteration, a new phase, new experiences and possibilities, release of the ego, liberation, cycles

- Apache Tear (Obsidian)
- Chrysocolla
- Labradorite
- Lepidolite
- Malachite
- Petrified Wood
- Smoky Quartz

Ask Yourself: Is there something in my life I need to let go? How can I grow based on releasing what I no longer need? What changes am I going though? Free yourself from whatever is holding you back from reaching your highest potential.

Magical Uses: release, easing transitions, transformation

14: Temperance

It's worth noting that the word temperance comes from the Latin *temperāre*, which means "to combine properly." I always think of the phrase "all things in moderation," when I encounter this card—avoiding extremes and seeking compromise when solving problems.

Key Words: moderation, a calm approach, understanding, navigating the "middle" path, harmony, balance, discipline, a combination of forces, patience and self-control, frugality, alchemical work, spiritual healing

- Amazonite

- Aquamarine

- Cat's Eye (cymophane)

- Celestite

- Herkimer Diamond

- Kyanite

- Jade

- Smoky Quartz

Ask Yourself: Do I feel balanced or do I act quickly, rashly, and with extremes? Do I overindulge in anything? How do I balance all aspects of my life—work, family, school, pleasure, etc.? How do I solve problems? Do I compromise with others? How do I react when challenged? Be optimistic and learn to "combine" well and cooperate.

Magical Uses: guidance, general balance, balancing the aura, healing, harmony, tolerance, understanding, cooperation

15: The Devil

Another one of the most ominous of the Major Arcana cards, the Devil is often as misunderstood as the Death card. On the journey through the cards, the Devil follows Temperance because we need the lessons learned from Temperance to confront our own "devils"—so we can avoid becoming trapped. On this stage of the journey, the soul is preparing to face great forces of the universe beyond human control. As in the archetypal Hero's Journey, the hero must descend into darkness before he can emerge into the light of victory and revelation. This is the first step on the next stage—we must face our fears and break the bonds in order to become strong enough for what lies ahead.

Key Words: illusion, confrontation, facing fears, breaking bonds, temptation

- Apache Tear (Obsidian)
- Chyrsocolla
- Jet
- Malachite
- Obsidian
- Quartz with Black Tourmaline
- Tourmaline (black)
- Topaz

Ask Yourself: What is holding me back? What are my fears? What boundaries do I face and how do I approach them? What are my limitations? Facing fears causes us to look within our deepest and darkest places—our hidden selves. Acknowledge this place; learn to change barriers into opportunities.

Magical Uses: breaking barriers, facing fears

16: The Tower

Here's another card that looks frightening, but is actually liberating. Building something new often requires the destruction of something that exists. On this inward journey, after experiencing the self-reflection and breaking of bonds, it's time to shake things up. This card can also represent revelations and new situations that can be beneficial. If we don't surrender to release, eventually it will happen anyway—and this could be painful. But, ultimately, we are set free.

Key Words: release, dramatic change or disruption, liberation, freedom, bouncing back, secrets revealed, change of beliefs or opinions, upheaval

- Fuchsite
- Malachite
- Zebra Rock

Ask Yourself: Have changes or upheavals in my life caused me pain or anger? How do I deal with this? Have any foundations in my life given way to instability? Have I experienced a sudden change? Seek the revelation that comes from surviving a difficult time. Hope is just around the corner.

Magical Uses: clearing obstacles, breaking bad habits, adapting to change

17: The Star

The release given from the Tower is found here—the calm that follows the storm. The Star represents hope. A great weight has been lifted. The clouds part and we can see the clear sky.

Key Words: hope, healing, optimism, new life, faith, guidance, satisfaction, renewal, peace, wishes granted

- Amazonite
- Amethyst
- Blue Lace Agate
- Milky Quartz
- Star Sapphire

Ask Yourself: What inspires me? What are my hopes and dreams? Have I received recognition for something? Celebrate who you are and be grateful for your gifts.

Magical Uses: cleansing, stress relief, purification, ritual and ceremony, meditation, spiritual guidance, freedom

18: The Moon

The journey is not finished. While the Fool may have been allowed to rest and have a moment of peace, there is still much to learn. Remember the lesson of the Hermit? Ultimately, after one gains knowledge, it needs to be shared with the world. The Fool must learn to do this. The soul has learned many lessons so far. The next step in this journey, after self-assessment, is a higher realm—intuition and imagination.

Key Words: instincts, dreams, myths, primal emotions, solitude, development of psychic powers, illusions, intuition, wisdom, possible deception

- Aquamarine
- Celestite
- Iolite
- Lavender Quartz
- Moonstone

Ask Yourself: What illusions do I cling to? Do I have the ability to recognize them? What confuses me? Do I listen to my instincts and insight? Learn to trust your inner guide. Face the unknown.

Magical Uses: dream magic, sleep, reveal mysteries, receptivity, concealment, past lives, astral travel, general magic

19: The Sun

After the Moon comes the Sun, as day follows night. This bright light of optimism represents success and happiness, time to shine, time to see things clearly and celebrate accomplishments.

Key Words: success, happiness, harmony, achievement, contentment, material success, sincerity, friendship

- Amber
- Aqua Aura Quartz
- Garnet
- Topaz

Ask Yourself: What goals have I reached? Am I celebrating success? Have I committed myself to goals? What have I learned and achieved? Am I energized and active? Do I pay attention to my health? Celebrate your moments in the sun. Be joyful and thankful. Realize your true worth and take care of yourself.

Magical Uses: energy, vitality, health, childbirth, combine with the Moon for balance, success, relaxation, creativity

20: Judgment

After learning wisdom and reaching maturity, the Fool arrives here—Judgment. But the Fool is not necessarily being judged. Instead, this card stands for a kind of return to life with a renewed sense of wonder and excitement. The Fool—the soul—sees the world with new eyes. Reap what you sow. This is a blending of spiritual wisdom, inner peace and balance, and an understanding of the world.

Key Words: wisdom, maturity, renewal, destiny, reflecting on the past, awareness, rebirth, second chances

- Purple Fluorite
- Star Sapphire
- Jade
- Lapis Lazuli

Ask Yourself: In what ways am I being judged or judging others? Am I fair? What are my responsibilities and how do I handle them? Have I experienced any rites of passage? How do I handle criticism? Do I know my purpose? Do I see the wonder and beauty in the world around me? Do I acknowledge it? Approach each new day with a renewed spirit.

Magical Uses: visualization, criticism, transformation and transition

21: *The World/Universe*

We have arrived at last. This card is the culmination of all parts of the journey—a new beginning, fulfillment. This is a state of deep understanding. We are all connected and that insight and wisdom is fulfilled here. It's the ultimate feeling of peace and harmony with the universe.

Key Words: fulfillment, culmination of a journey, ultimate goal, completion, reward, wholeness, joy, spiritual connection and wonder

- Blue Lace Agate
- Clear Quartz
- Opal
- Sapphire
- Chevron Amethyst
- Lavender Quartz

Ask Yourself: Do I recognize my potential? What makes me happy? Do I feel fulfilled? Do I see my connection with others and the world—the connection of all things in the universe? Do I act accordingly, with love, humility, patience, and joy? What life lessons have I learned? What still needs attention? Know that you are in this world for a reason and that you deserve joy and abundance.

Magical Uses: psychic protection, connections, insight, new beginnings, journeys

Spells and Spell Techniques

Before providing specific spells, here are some basic techniques you can use to customize your own spell or meditation.

One very simple way to combine tarot cards and crystals is to pick the card first, based on your need, or use a card you drew at random or received in a reading. Select appropriate stones from the corresponding list and place them near the card on your altar or other place where you will see them each day. You can create a meditation altar, or create a spell based on the properties of the card and stone. To do this, consider all the various properties of both the card and the stone when creating your spell—which elements are associated with it? How does it relate to your personal life? Use the key words and questions listed for each card. Read over the metaphysical properties of the stone(s) in the appendix and see if any of those characteristics are relevant to you at this time. The card and stone(s) can then be used together as you either take action or meditate to receive guidance.

You can also find your personal card and choose stones that resonate with it. One way to do this is to calculate your birth number by adding together all the numbers in your birthday before reducing them down to a single digit—for example, January 1, 1988 would be 1+1+1+9+8+8 = 28; 2+8 = 10; 1+0 = 1. In this case, your birth number is 1 but since 10 is also a tarot card number, both the Magician (1) and the Wheel of Fortune (10) cards could hold special significance for you. Consider also incorporating your natal stone or personal power stone, as discussed in *The Book of Crystal Spells*. There are many tarot books that contain other ways to determine cards that could be of particular use—including calculations for specific years, cards associated with your astrological sign, and more. I encourage you to use crystals as you investigate these various tarot card uses.

There are so many varieties of decks and meditation cards that exist—the deck you use could have many subtle differences from the classic card traits described here. Consult the book that accompanied your deck, if possible, for variations, then choose a stone from the appendix.

Simple Spell Guidelines

Here's a basic outline for creating a tarot and crystal spell or meditation altar that still allows plenty of personal freedom.

Choose the appropriate moon phase and/or moon sign, day of the week, etc., as desired and create your sacred space. Place the card on your altar or other special location where it will not be disturbed. Select a stone (or stones) from the corresponding list and set the stone on top of the card. (If your stone has rough edges, place a small piece of cloth under it so it won't scratch the card.) If you have several stones, create a circle around the card. If you have a very large stone, you can prop the card against it. You can also create a grid around the card based on numerology using stones or quartz points (see chapter five). For example, since the Lovers is card number six, you could select six stones and arrange them around the card in a balanced way—three on each side.

Imagine the energy of the card and stone combining and visualize your specific goal. Say appropriate words if you choose. If you seek to embody a quality the card symbolizes, see yourself in the card. Imagine the scene in the picture all around you. Do this for as long as you need before completing your ritual. Burn appropriate candles and incense if you wish.

Leave the arrangement on your altar as long as you like, or create a separate space to leave your layout in place for several months, if necessary. Depending on your goal, you may wish to carry the stone(s) with you. For example, some cards (and crystals) are simply too large to carry conveniently—unless you have one of those miniature decks! One way to keep the image in mind throughout the day is to tape the card in a visible place— a bulletin board, the refrigerator, etc. Use a magnet or removable sticky tape to avoid damaging the card. If you prefer an elaborate altar layout, or have large crystals, leave the card and stone(s) but designate at least one small stone you can carry with you or incorporate a piece of jewelry into the spell so you can wear it. Also consider placing the card beneath your mattress and the stone in your pillowcase, especially if your goal involves dreaming.

Spell for Strength: A Template

Here's an example of how you can create a spell based on your need using a specific card and the corresponding stones. The Strength card has a variety of interpretations. Let's say, in this case, I want to boost my confidence and creativity to explore a new project. The key associations I'd like to draw from this card are courage, determination, and creativity.

I begin by placing the card on my altar. Since 8 is the number of the Strength card, I'll use 8 clear quartz points and choose stones from this list: Hemimorphite, Rutilated Quartz, Tiger Eye, Sodalite, Smoky Quartz. To make this as personal as possible, I would choose Hemimorphite and Smoky Quartz because they're associated with my sun sign. Additionally, I would add a Rutilated Quartz pendant to wear after the spell is complete. The properties of this stone include inspiration and clearing the way for progress, which are perfect for my specific goals.

You can arrange the items in whatever way appeals to you. I place the pendant on the card, then create a circle of quartz points around the card, facing inward, to charge the pendant. Incorporate candles or incense as desired. Meditate on the card's meaning and the qualities you desire for at least ten minutes. Because I'm so fond of chants, I would say a few words like this:

> *Courage to explore and seek,*
> *when I write and when I speak—*
> *help me find the strength I need*
> *for this project to succeed.*

Or, if you want to use the spell for boosting your inner strength or to deal with balancing emotions, you could chant:

I am balanced, I am strong,
help me find where I belong.

I like to use candles or incense to have a way to mark the spell completion. When the candle(s) or incense burns out, the spell is complete—the pendant is charged and ready to wear. I would leave the altar arrangement in place for about a week. This, again, is up to you.

Meditation to Enhance Magical Practice

Place a piece of Wulfenite on or near the Magician card. Visualize yourself connecting with the universe and tapping into your personal power. How does this make you feel? What can you accomplish? What does this version of you look like—are you more confident? Happier? Peaceful? More energetic? Keep taking steps toward improving your skills. Read and study. Meditate. Use this card and stone as a reminder of your dedication. Spend time each day working toward your goals. Try this chant:

Each day I grow in wisdom, becoming more adept—
this knowledge and responsibility I do accept.
I polish my skill, I strengthen my will—
with dedication I become aware.
Let me not forget.

The Fool: Opportunity Spell

For this spell, carry or wear a piece of soapstone. This is intended to pave the way for new opportunities to come your way—and for you to be ready and willing to receive them. For this spell to work, you must truly and sincerely be open to new experiences, even though they may present challenges and result in change.

Visualize and place the stone on or near the card, then carry or wear the stone. Chant:

I am open, I am willing,
new adventure, come to me.
I am ready, I am seeking,
something new that's good for me.

The Chariot: Manifestation Spell

For this spell you will need a very special type of quartz point called a Manifestation Crystal (see chapter three). If you don't have one, just use a clear quartz point or any combination of the crystals associated with the Chariot card.

Perform this spell during a waxing or full moon phase—choose the appropriate moon sign based on your needs.

Place the stone on or near the card, lighting a candle if you wish. First, visualize and say out loud what you wish to manifest. Are you seeking a new career, developing new skills, looking for love, a new home, or education? Are you working on a project, overcoming an obstacle, or hoping for abundance and success? Be as specific as you can. See it happening in your mind. Chant:

That which I seek shall manifest
for me in the way that's best.

Carry the stone with you or keep it where you can see it each day. In addition, be sure the card is visible each day as well.

Tarot Elemental Spells and Meditations

Each of these spells and meditations uses the Ace card of the suit. Choose stones from the list provided for each of the four elements and place the stones around the card (or on it); meditate on the qualities of the element as you visualize your specific need or goal. An optional chant is provided for each. These spells can be used to tap into the qualities of each particular elemental energy.

Elemental Associations

This list was compiled, like most lists in this book, by cross-referencing at least half a dozen sources. Many stones are too new in metaphysical usage and don't have such associations as we can find in folklore. Therefore, if you feel that a particular stone is associated with a certain element, but it's not listed here (or you simply disagree with its classification), go with it. Use your instinct. For unclassified rocks, you can base your decision on the minerals that make up the stone. Or, you can decide based on color.

Earth: amazonite, agate (especially dendritic, moss, and tree), amber, bronzite, calcite (especially green), green jasper, emerald, fossils of plants and land animals, galena, granite, malachite, olivine (peridot), onyx, jet, salt, tourmaline (green and black), turquoise, petrified wood, clear quartz

Air: mica, aventurine, fluorite, fuchsite, opal, pewter, pumice, tin, topaz

Fire: amber, brass, bloodstone, carnelian, citrine, diamond, fire opal, garnet, gold, hematite, iron, obsidian (Apache tear), pyrite, pyrolusite, ruby, rhodocrosite, rhodonite, sulfur, tangerine quartz, tiger eye, topaz, zircon

Water: amethyst, aquamarine, azurite, celestite, chrysocolla, copper, blue lace agate, geodes, jade, labradorite, lapis lazuli, lepidolite, lodestone, moonstone, pearl, platinum, sapphire, silver, sodalite, blue tourmaline, fossils of sea animals, and shells

Chalice Meditation—Water Element

In Irish folklore, the cauldron was a common magical symbol. Some believe this may be the source of the grail stories of Arthurian legend. In magical practice, the cup and cauldron symbolize water, the womb, and the goddess, as well as regeneration, calm, and healing. Water has long been associated with creation (as well as destruction). Many creation stories in mythology begin with water.

Getting in touch with the element of water can help you with creativity, emotions, intuition, cleansing, dream issues, and sensuality. It's receptive, so if you feel the need to increase this quality in your life, work with the water element. Water is also associated with the moon, the sense of taste, the season of autumn, and the middle-age stage of life.

Use the Ace of Cups and any of the stones associated with the water element.

> *Bowl and chalice, cup and cauldron*
> *water running, rivers flow—*
> *deepest wells and shallow puddles*
> *falling rain and drifting snow.*
> *Lakes and oceans, ponds and springs*
> *womb of life and restless tides,*
> *water of the world embrace me*
> *where the mystery resides.*

Wand Spell—Fire Element

Rods, wands, and staves are the magical tools associated with the element of fire. These are the items that most commonly come to mind when one pictures a magician. The wand is an instrument of change and transformation, as is the element of fire. Use the Ace of Wands/Rods card for this spell. Fire is transformative—it's used in magic for change, power, purification, strength, and courage. The energy of fire is projective; it's associated with the season of summer, the sense of sight, and youthfulness. Fire is the realm of passion.

Use this spell to bring out the qualities of fire for transformation or change. Additionally, you can use this for charging a wand.

> *Flames of fire dancing bright,*
> *stirring heat, the spark of life—*
> *let your power now ignite.*

Sword Spell—Air Element

The tools of the air element are the dagger and sword. Air is associated with birth, the season of spring, and the sense of smell. Air rules magic for the intellect and the mind. Like fire, air is projective. Use air magic for all aspects of communication, learning, and studying. It's also excellent for symbolizing new beginnings.

> *Raging wind and gentle breeze,*
> *breath of air with force or ease—*
> *swirling air bring expertise.*

Pentacle Meditation—Earth Element

In the tarot, earth is associated with the suit of pentacles. The earth element rules aspects of the material world, the body, sensations, growth and abundance, and things of a practical nature. Earth is associated with the sense of touch, the season of winter, and old age. Like water, earth is receptive and sometimes associated with nurturing and healing (think Mother Earth). Since earth is associated with old age and death, it may seem that earth is cold and unyielding, but this is not the case. It's where things grow. Earth represents the cycle of life—things grow in earth and return to it.

> *Deep within the earth,*
> *the home of sleeping seeds,*
> *soil, roots, and stones—*
> *earth, fulfill our needs.*

Fifth Element Spell

The pentacle symbol has further magical significance, as you most likely already know. The four classical elements and the spirit are each associated with a point on the pentagram. Therefore, you can also use the Ace of Pentacles for other spells and meditations, not just earth magic. Spirit, also called Akasha (Sanskrit) is associated with the sense of hearing and the entire wheel of the year. Forms of light such as lamps and candles are also symbolic of the spirit. To get in touch with the spirit, or all the elements, use a clear quartz point or Spirit Quartz (see chapter three).

> *Fire, water, earth, and air—*
> *let my senses be aware.*
> *Spirit, fill me with your light,*
> *all the elements unite—*
> *balance of the dark and light.*

Court Card Correspondences

Court cards typically suggest a particular type of personality. For these meditations, choose a card that represents a quality you desire to possess.

Or, you can choose a card based on an archetype—for example, use one of the queen cards to serve as a mother figure or a king as a father figure. Perhaps you're seeking a mentor or you will be in a mentoring role yourself—be as specific as you can when focusing on your need.

Traditionally, the court cards represent the following traits. Keep in mind there is a great deal of variety in these card personalities, depending on the deck you use. I have selected stones that I believe to be good personality matches for each particular characteristic; you can also choose stones from the list of elemental associations earlier in this chapter—the element that corresponds to each card plays a role in each character's symbolic meaning. You can also use your personal power stone or natal stone, if you wish. Use the stone that feels right for you.

- **Page**—a young person, either of youthful spirit, or a child; a student; eagerness
  - » *Fire/Wands:* ready to try new things; playful
    - Bornite, Citrine
  - » *Water/Cups:* dreamy; psychic development
    - Azurite, Moonstone, Sodalite
  - » *Air/Swords:* alert and intelligent
    - Yellow Fluorite
  - » *Earth/Pentacles:* ideal student; appreciation of environment and nature
    - Agate; Calcite
- **Knight**—idealistic; an adolescent; someone on the verge of self-discovery; adventurous spirit; taking action
  - » *Fire/Wands:* adventurous and energetic
    - Bloodstone, Carnelian

» *Water/Cups:* dreams and imagination; possibly reluctant

  – Jade, Lepidolite

» *Air/Swords:* courageous—ready to take charge

  – Aventurine, Aquamarine

» *Earth/Pentacles:* acceptance of responsibility or desire to escape

  – Iolite, Septarian Nodule

• **Queen**—maturity; inspiration and appreciation of life; a woman; someone with a gentle touch

» *Fire/Wands:* confident and powerful

  – Topaz

» *Water/Cups:* loving and sensual

  – Chrysocolla, Unakite

» *Air/Swords:* independent, decisive, and truthful

  – Apophyllite

» *Earth/Pentacles:* prosperous and happy

  – Amazonite, Gypsum, Jasper

• **King**—power and wisdom; responsibility, knowledge, and mastery; a man

» *Fire/Wands:* powerful and strong-willed

  – Bloodstone, Tiger Eye, Tiger Iron

» *Water/Cups:* emotional and artistic

  – Lodestone, Picasso Stone

» *Air/Swords:* authoritative and intelligent

  – Vanadinite

» *Earth/Pentacles:* successful and proud

    – Aragonite, Granite

Court Card Meditation

So now that you've matched a card with a stone (or stones), what's next? You can use the Simple Spell Guidelines in this chapter to design a spell or altar layout. Carefully consider the card you've chosen (or drawn at random). Are these qualities you have or need? Are they qualities that are deficient, or that you seek to enhance? This kind of soul-searching can be difficult and time-consuming. Be patient. Daily meditation can help—focus on the card's image while holding the crystal(s) in your receptive hand.

Decks and Readings

You can use corresponding stones before, during, and after a reading to aid insight and focus or to protect and purify your deck. Clear quartz is always a good option, but you can choose a stone of awareness instead to intensify your skills (see chapter 7). Clear quartz amplifies the energy of other stones, so select a collection of stones and keep them with your deck. You can also hold stones in your hand before a reading to help you focus. Keep them on the table while you read; use them for grounding after a reading.

Post-Reading Meditation

Perhaps you've been confused or unsure about cards you received in a reading. Contemplating what message(s) the card(s) hold can be difficult. Often we're told to meditate on this—but how should we approach this process? Here's a ritual you can use to get started.

Whether it's a single card or an elaborate layout, sit before the cards and study them. Gain what meaning you can from the cards first and their position in the layout (if applicable). Then examine the list in this chapter that contains key words and questions associated with the cards. As you're looking at the list, see if any of the corresponding stones appeal to you and, for the ones you choose, read more about the properties of that stone (or stones). See if any information about the stones resonates with you.

You can either create a display on your altar that combines the selected card(s) and stones or choose stones to wear or carry with you. Whichever you choose, first spend time considering the implications of both the cards and stones. Perhaps choose a special quartz point from chapter three or an intuitive stone from chapter seven and use those to help gain insight on the interpretation.

Light a candle near the cards and stones you've chosen, close your eyes, and chant:

Message from the cards, message from the stones—
make it clear to me, what I need to know.

- THREE -

SPECIAL QUARTZ POINTS

Similar to my chapter on special quartz points in *The Book of Crystal Spells*, this chapter explores specific shapes that some quartz points or clusters can display. This time, the focus is on the overall appearance (shape or color) of the crystal rather than on the number of sides on a particular crystal face. These interesting appearances are the result of unusual growth formations or the presence of other minerals that cause the stone to display a particular color.

Remember that these terms are not always scientific or used in geological study. Sometimes a term refers to the appearance or is simply used to describe the stone; other times the name refers to metaphysical properties—sometimes both.

There simply isn't room here to discuss the hundreds of varieties that exist. The ones I chose are stones I have personally worked with and that appear to be easily obtainable (with a few exceptions). The bibliography lists some informative websites—many also include helpful photos of these formations. My effort here is to offer you specific ways to use these interesting crystals in your spellwork or meditation practice.

It's possible that you will find a quartz point that displays several of these characteristics. You may have a point that is both a Trigger and a Bridge, for example. One of the Aqua Aura points I have is also a Key, and my Lavender Quartz Point is also a Sprouting Point. Points like these combine all the features of the characteristics they display.

There can be some overlap in descriptions, and there will always be stones that simply defy any name or category. Do some research and see where yours fits best. Odd formations like Elestial, Sprouting, and Fenster/Skeletal can be confusing and difficult to describe. And, depending on the source, these names are used in different ways or grouped together. It can be confusing. When in doubt, try to locate some photos and, ultimately, trust your personal judgment.

Barnacle

Barnacle
Quartz

These points feature places that are partially covered with smaller crystal chips or tiny points, sometimes forming a type of crust over the stone's surface. This crust can cover only one side of the crystal or many sides (not to be confused with the Spirit Crystal, which is completely covered by tiny crystal points). The covering on Barnacle Points is usually somewhat chaotic in appearance and can also include etching (see Etched Quartz).

Barnacles are excellent meditation crystals; they can help you gain insight, especially in dealing with family and community issues, and are excellent for people in service professions. Like a cluster, they can facilitate group work. This crystal can also aid one in dealing with loss.

Allow your Barnacle Crystal to sit in full moon light for an entire evening. Prepare for meditation as usual and visualize your goal while holding the stone in your receptive hand. It may sound silly, but talk to the crystal. Explain your situation and the answers you seek. Proceed with meditation. Hold the crystal each time you meditate for answers regarding your situation. Think of it as asking the crystal for advice. Repeated use for the same purpose will continually improve your results.

Bridge

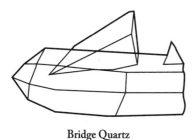

Bridge Quartz

This type of crystal point has another point partially penetrating it; part of a crystal seems to have grown into a larger crystal while the rest remains outside. This crystal can create a "bridge" between inner and outer worlds, as well as helping you connect with others. It fosters understanding and communication, helps with introducing new ideas and concepts, and is useful for teaching and spiritual pursuits. Some sources have another classification called the "Inner Child" which seems similar to the Bridge—in this case, the penetrating crystal has grown more deeply inside the main crystal. This type can help you get in touch with your youthful spirit and childlike awe that you may have lost.

Bridge Quartz Connection Spell

Visualize whatever specific goal you have while holding the stone; chant three times: *Here to there, connect and share.* Hold the stone in your projective hand to send energy toward something or someone; use your receptive hand to aid your own understanding and response to a situation. Charge this crystal in sunlight for clarity of communication and expression—to make your message crystal-clear. After the stone has been in direct sunlight for several hours, repeat the visualization and chant.

Drusy Quartz

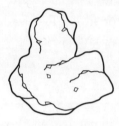

Drusy Quartz

In geological terms, druse (drusy or druzy) is a crust of many tiny crystals on the surface of a stone. It's very common; in fact, when I was a child these were some of the first types of stones I found. These pieces are not crystals themselves—they are most often found as bulbous-shaped rocks or rounded masses with a layer of tiny crystals over them, like a coating or carpet. This formation can occur in other types of minerals, not just quartz.

Drusy Quartz can be used to help remove negativity and create an uplifting atmosphere. With their thousands and thousands of tiny crystal points, they can easily bring sparkle to any area—indoors or out. These are my favorite stones to add to the garden or potted plants. There is a recent trend of creating jewelry from pieces of Drusy Quartz. In fact, you can use Drusy Quartz like you would use a quartz cluster—to bring a calming atmosphere to a room. They're wonderful accents for a family room or places where many people gather—like offices or places of business. Here's a spell to charge your Drusy Quartz for bringing calm, positive energy to a room.

Drusy Quartz Room Spell

First, cleanse your stone under running water. You can use a faucet or hose, hold it in a running stream, or just pour water over it. Visualize the water clearing away any negative energy and, instead, refreshing the stone to enhance the specific qualities you wish to promote. Speak those qualities aloud. Allow the stone to dry naturally in sunlight.

CHANT:

Sparkle, shimmer, glimmer, glow—
peaceful energy will flow.

Elestial

This fascinating formation is recognized by a kind of layering or clustering of many points and faces together—they usually generate from one main base or form in a mass. An online search will yield a wide variety of descriptions and photos.

Elestial ("heavenly") is a metaphysical term for this layered type of quartz growth pattern. Some people in the mineral community call the Fenster Quartz by this term

Elestial Quartz

as well, but let's distinguish these—Fenster Quartz has a skeletal appearance on the inside; the outside is usually smooth. Elestial points have the appearance of many jumbled crystal faces, producing an almost scalelike appearance—which has earned them the name Jacare or Jacari (from the Portuguese word for alligator) in an attempt to describe this unique formation. The term Jacare is best applied to the Elestial that contains many defined faces without natural, terminating points. Think of how you might imagine dragon scales to look. There are some stones that do display characteristics of both Fenster and Elestial, but these are rare. Some stones called Elestial are actually Sprouting Quartz.

Elestials are sometimes called "goddess crystals" because they tend to be quite useful for women. They are especially powerful, containing lots of energy, and are excellent for use in leadership positions. The Jacare type can enhance persuasiveness, effectiveness, and community work, and help clear blocked energy. It can stimulate the chakras and ease blockages.

Also an excellent third-eye stone, it can also assist with clairaudience, clairvoyance, and clairsentience.

You may find the energy of these crystals to be "busy"—a bit confusing and chaotic. To calm the energy a bit, charge your Elestial or Jacare in moonlight on a bed of sea salt. To take full advantage of its forceful personality, charge it in bright, intense sunlight. You may wish to meditate with your stone to find the purpose for which it's best suited.

Etched

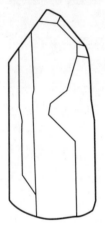

Etched Quartz

At first glance, an Etched Crystal may appear to have been deeply scratched or scraped. Rest assured it is not damaged; this is yet another natural feature of crystal formation. During the crystal's growth, sometimes other minerals dissolve part of the quartz or certain geologic conditions cause disruptions in the crystal's structure. When the stone is severely etched, it is sometimes called Corroded.

Crystals are considered Etched if their markings are not perfectly formed pyramids or faces, as with Record Keepers or Elestials; nor are they distinct shapes as in the Key formation. These markings are not straight lines, either, as in the Striated Quartz. Of course, all these types can certainly occur together. The abrasions can be deep and rough or light and scaly. They can be on one or more sides of the crystal, or even on the faces. They can take the form of odd shapes, pits, jagged lines, or be so severe that the quartz point scarcely retains its crystal shape.

The markings on Etched Crystals make them especially useful for scrying or gazing. As with many other special quartz points, these are also good mediation stones; they can also be used to stimulate the third-eye chakra. Trace or rub the markings with your finger as you meditate; look for patterns in your crystal that may reveal its purpose for you.

Faden

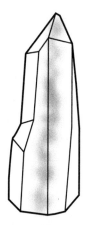

The Faden Crystal has a milky white, opaque, feathery line that runs through the crystal. This formation occurs often (but not exclusively) in Tabby Crystals. It's pronounced *fah*-den; the name comes from the German word Faden-quarz—*faden* means "thread." This formation is believed to occur when a crystal is repeatedly ruptured and healed during its formation. This results in a type of scar due to inclusions of water or gases.

Faden Quartz

One of the main properties of the Faden is connection and attunement with others; it has been reputed to help one find compatible companions. It can also aid in seeking information. Other uses include astral travel, aura cleansing, opening chakras, and psychic ability, as well as stability and centering.

Faden Quartz Seeker's Spell

Write what you seek on a slip of paper and wrap the paper around your Faden Quartz. Visualize the thread inside the stone linking you to what you seek. Place the stone and paper in a small dish or jar, and fill the jar with enough sand or salt to fill the container, covering the paper-wrapped crystal. Place the dish on your altar or in another special place for an entire moon cycle (one month). Begin the spell on a full moon and end just as the moon becomes full again.

Fairy

See the entry on Spirit Quartz for more information.

Fenster

Fenster Quartz

The Fenster Quartz is one of the most unusual and striking crystal formations. These are also sometimes called Skeletal Quartz or Window Quartz. The name comes from the German word Fensterquarz, which means "window," and describes the peculiar growth pattern of these crystals. Fenster Points are filled with chambers and pockets of air; because of all the air pockets, they actually feel lighter in your hand. They are smooth on the outside but inside they appear to have many layers of windows. In fact, the largest one in my collection has a very small opening so you can actually see the space between the crystal layers. The type of crystal most often called Skeletal, on the other hand, has little triangular windows in the main crystal faces of the point; they are not smooth on the outside like Fenster Crystals.

The interesting appearance of these stones is believed to be caused by sudden temperature or pressure changes during the crystal's formation. As water drains away, leaving behind bubbles, chambers, and pockets remain, causing a skeletal appearance inside the crystal. Sometimes materials or water become trapped in the pockets (causing another nickname, Water Quartz). Fenster Crystals occur in a variety of shapes and interesting forms—the type of crystals that are rough on the surface, lacking a smooth outer appearance, are called Hopper Crystals. These crystals often display rainbow effects as well, and can form in stacked patterns.

Fenster Points can be single- or double-terminated and typically have an extremely brilliant appearance due to the all the internal layers. These crystals can be found in several places around the world—one of the most popular areas is Mexico. Additionally, Fenster Points can be found in the Herkimer District of New York—the geologic conditions that produce the famous Herkimer Diamonds can also cause these growth forms. However, they can't truly be called Herkimer Diamonds, since Herkimer Diamonds are known for being flawless or nearly flawless.

Use Fenster Quartz for insight into yourself and the world around you; you can use Skeletal Quartz in the same way. Here's a technique for gazing or scrying using one of these stones.

Fenster Quartz Window Meditation

Think of all these layers, these windows, as a way to see more deeply into areas that need your attention—these could be aspects of yourself, or a situation. Visualize what you need and imagine the layers of windows opening, one after another, as you go deeper and deeper.

CHANT:
Window to the world I seek, let me take a deeper peek.

Key

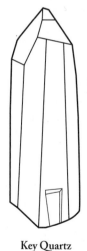

Key Quartz

The Key Crystal contains one or more 3- or 6-sided indentations on the side of the stone, like keyholes to "unlock" doors to your hidden self, inner self, or other secrets. Use this stone for problem solving, studying, or seeking the answer to a dilemma.

Key Crystal Meditation

Dedicate or charge this stone during a waxing or full moon phase, ideally when the moon is in the sign of Aquarius or Pisces. Hold the stone between your clasped hands, and visualize your problem or dilemma as a door—the answer lies on the other side.

Imagine the crystal is the key; see yourself opening the door. Or, if you prefer, see yourself walking into the key shape in the side of the stone and entering a realm of understanding.

CHANT:
I hold the key, unlock the door—
reveal to me, show me more.

Laser Wand

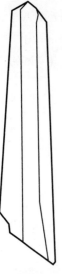

Laser Wand Crystals are long and thin, and they taper, often dramatically, toward the point; the narrowing of the crystal should be clearly distinct for it to be classified as a Laser Wand. The faces on the tip are typically quite small. Some of these are thin enough to also be classified as Singing Quartz, and so the crystal contains properties of both.

Use Laser Wand Crystals to fine-tune your meditation or to send focused energy to a specific area. Use them like a tiny wand, adding precision to your magic. A protective barrier can be established by using the Laser Wand to direct the removal of negativity.

Laser Wand
Quartz

Laser Wand Cleansing Ritual

Before you begin, be sure your crystal has been properly cleansed and charged or dedicated for its purpose; for this ritual, I recommend charging it in full sunlight. Visualize your Laser Wand Crystal as an actual laser beam, destroying negative energy wherever you point it. You can combine this spell with the Banishing Elixir from chapter one if you'd like. For best results, perform this ritual during a waning moon phase. When you point the crystal, visualize negativity dissolving, being burned away. Say the words *dissolve, be clear,* each time you focus your energy on a specific area. See the negativity, barriers, or whatever you wish to remove, disappearing right before your eyes.

Manifestation

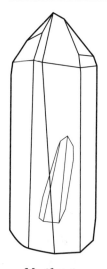

Manifestation
Quartz

These points have another entire crystal contained completely within them. Often these resemble a Bridge Crystal but, in this case, the larger crystal has completely covered the smaller one. The crystal inside is usually quite small. These are rare.

I have one Manifestation Crystal and it's an amethyst. It's only about an inch long. Like many of my most special crystals, this one came to me by chance—I didn't seek it out or choose it. My husband accompanied me to a rock and mineral show, spotted this brilliant little amethyst point that appeared to have many sparkling inclusions, and said, simply, "I like this one." I agreed, and bought it. It was only later that I discovered its secret. What I thought were just inclusions turned out to be much more! Inside the point of the crystal there is another, very tiny, horizontal crystal point. I had to use a magnifying glass to be sure I wasn't imagining it. There's also a little triangle in there, too—it looks like an internal Record Keeper. Such an impressive stone!

The Manifestation Crystal has a question for you—what do you need to manifest in your life? And, what do you need to do in order to accomplish your goal? Do you really want what you think you want? (See the Crystals and Tarot chapter for a Manifestation Spell.)

You can also use Manifestation Crystals to increase optimism, wonder, and creativity. I like to keep mine on my altar, where I can see it, or hold it when I meditate.

Phantom

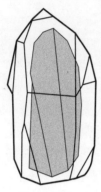

A Phantom Quartz Crystal has what *appears* to be another crystal (or crystals) within it. I say "appears" because, unlike the Manifestation Crystal, these are sometimes not actual crystals—they're often "ghostlike" shapes or shadows that look like another crystal.

The "phantom" can be partial or complete, and can either be a single point or a pattern of several chevronlike shapes. They are aligned with the host crystal—pointing in the same direction.

Phantom Quartz

Phantoms form in two main ways. Sometimes a crystal actually grows over another one; the crystal inside can even be a different shape or color than the outer one. In this case, there really is a crystal inside another crystal. These are somewhat rare.

The "stacked" type of phantom with the chevron shapes occurs when inclusions of minerals change at various times during the crystal's growth. Environmental conditions during the crystal's growth can also cause phantoms to form. Sometimes a crystal stops growing and then starts again. These are the most common types of phantom.

Use these points for universal awareness, earth healing, meditation, and to reach higher realms of knowledge and self-understanding. They can also assist you in meeting and communicating with your spirit guides and can aid clairaudience.

Phantom Crystal Dedication

Dedicate your Phantom Crystal during the full moon. If possible, place it outside within a ring of white candles and allow the candles to burn out. As you light the candles, visualize your specific goal. To use your crystal, hold it in either your receptive or projective hand, depending on your purpose, and chant: *Phantom stone of mystery, serve the goal I set for thee.*

"Reversed" Record Keeper

"Reversed"
Record Keeper
Quartz

As I spend more time examining my crystals, I always find new markings—most recently, I've been researching "Reversed" Record Keeper points. There are two ways to define these. First, the one I noticed on one of my stones—the tiny triangular marking is recessed instead of being raised. Also, this marking is turned on its side instead of facing upward.

There's another type of unusual Record Keeper called Trigonic or Trigon (not to be confused with Trigonal structure). These are even more rare than standard Record Keepers. Like the Record Keeper, these crystals have small triangles on one or more of the crystal faces; however, in this case, the triangles point in the opposite direction of the crystal point. Some crystals contain triangles that face both directions.

I'm starting to think Record Keepers aren't really rare. I have about a dozen and I keep finding them. On the other hand, of the hundreds of clear quartz points I have now, I have yet to find a Trigonic. I'm thrilled, however, to have the recessed Record Keeper, and I've been experimenting with ways to use it.

Both of these reversed types of Record Keepers can be used like the traditional ones—they are excellent meditation stones and have been reputed to aid spiritual pursuits. On those that display triangles facing both directions, if a majority face upward, the stone is best suited for mental activities; if most triangles face downward, it is said to be connected strongly to the element of fire. Those with points all facing down are said to help the user gain an understanding of the afterlife. Unfortunately, at this time, I am unable to offer my personal experience with these stones. However, I would like to comment on the "Recessed" Record Keeper since it's also very unusual.

The "Recessed" Record Keeper has properties of both the Record Keeper and the Key. This unique pairing gives the stone a very distinct energy. Meditating with crystals like these is not always the relaxing experience people seek. In fact, the stone often seems to almost hum with untapped potential that's eager to escape.

Here are some techniques to try.

Gazing is more than merely looking at your crystal—it's something like scrying. Look into the depth of the crystal to understand it and get to know its personality. Each stone is different and studying them helps you attune to their energy. Try a variety of light settings—use bright indoor light, sunlight, and candlelight. Use a magnifying glass. Close your eyes and sense the crystal. How does it feel in your hand? Switch hands and see if you can feel a difference. Note any raised markings or striations you can feel—even tiny trigger points. Ask for guidance. See if the stone has a message for you.

If you find a "Reversed" Record Keeper, find ways to connect with it. Listen to what it tells you; try to understand the reason it came to you. This could be one of your most personal crystal magic experiences.

Scepter

Scepter points look like a rod with a capped point on top; some resemble mushrooms. They are often used as phallic symbols. In the Reversed Scepter formation, the crystal on the tip is smaller instead of larger than the parent crystal. Other types display a stacked formation. In this case, instead of a rodlike base, there is another fully developed crystal point growing on top of another crystal that was developing into a point of its own, and sometimes a fully formed crystal is attached on the side of another (see Stacked).

These stones are excellent for focusing and directing energy. They are often used for spiritual pursuits and healing—think of them like a pointer, directing you to areas that need attention. These crystals can also be used as a tool for seeking answers, especially during meditation.

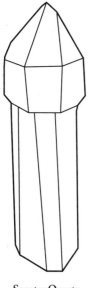

Scepter Quartz

Scepter Crystal Meditation

Hold the scepter crystal in your projective hand and visualize it like an arrow, a way to point you in the direction you seek. Whisper your question or speak it aloud. Ask for guidance as you seek the answer or resolution. Then, switch the crystal to your receptive hand.

CHANT:

Be my guide—answers are inside.

Repeat this meditation daily, knowing you will discover what you need. You already have the answer within you, you just need to find it.

Sheet

Sheet Quartz can also be called Lens Quartz. It's a flat or thin layer of clear quartz. This type of quartz can be used as a window to your inner self, to other dimensions, or for scrying. Useful for the third eye chakra, it can help stimulate psychic abilities and visions.

Sheet Quartz

Sheet Quartz Second Sight Meditation

To stimulate your "second sight," find a place in bright, direct sunlight, if possible. Sit with the sun at your back, and hold the stone so light illuminates it. You can also try this with moonlight or candlelight, but natural sunlight typically works best. Gazing upon the crystal, gradually bring it closer and closer to your eyes, letting them go into a soft focus (as when scrying). Chant: *Second Sight, come to light* (repeat as desired). For more on stones associated with the "sixth sense," see chapter seven.

Shovel

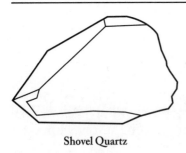

Shovel Quartz

This type of quartz point has one very long, steep face that causes the point to look unbalanced. Like the Sheet Quartz, the Shovel can help you find solutions and resolve problems. This particular stone can help you make sense of lessons learned—both good and bad.

During the time I wrote this book, I only had one Shovel Quartz Point. Then, about a month before I completed writing, I obtained a Lithium Quartz Point that is also a Shovel Point (this point has Key properties as well). The clarity of this point is nearly perfect, but there are some chips and imperfections on the surface. Remember to look past those flaws when working with crystals. Like us, they're not perfect. But each has something special to offer.

Shovel Quartz Meditation

As with the Scepter Crystal, meditate with this stone while focusing on what you seek. Run one of your fingers (or your thumb) down the steep face of the crystal, toward the point, as you focus on what you seek. Remember to have a specific focus, or you could be overwhelmed. Like digging in the dirt, the Shovel can reveal more than you anticipated finding. Be prepared to dig up unresolved issues with this stone.

Singing

The Singing Crystal is a long, thin point and makes a clear, sweet sound when gently tapped against another crystal—especially another Singing Crystal.

These can be used to connect with your higher self, to dissolve energy blocks, and to clear the aura. Don't confuse these with Laser Wand Crystals, which are more than just long, narrow points—they have a distinctive tapering toward the end.

I have one Singing Quartz Crystal in my collection and it's quite small.

Unfortunately, I did not obtain two of them, but the Singing Crystal will still make its signature sound when tapped against another crystal—it doesn't have to be another Singing Point, but the sound is best if both crystals are long and thin.

Singing Quartz

I like to think of these crystals as reset buttons. Like the sound of a bell that clears the air, the sound these crystals make can clear negativity from your aura, or a room, and even help you prepare for meditation or ritual.

Singing Quartz Affirmation

Dedicate your Singing Crystal during a full moon. Allow the stone to soak up the moonlight all night, if possible. Then, holding the stone in your cupped palms, gently breathe on it several times, like you're blowing out a candle. Close your eyes. Visualize your breath making a connection between you and the crystal—your voice engaging with the voice of the crystal. Repeat three times. Next, make the crystal sing, and say these words: *Crystal sing, as you ring, when I hear, all is clear.*

Spiral

Spiral Quartz Points have a slightly twisted appearance—they appear to curve in an almost spiraling formation. This crystal fosters a connection with the physical world during mediation while adding a spiral of energy, stimulating awareness. Like the Singing Quartz, it can be used to remove energy blockage and can also be effective when used to activate the Kundalini. It can also activate the chakras and is said to enhance one's balance—both with subtle energies and physically. It's like the Singing Quartz, but with more energy. My Singing Point is also a Spiral (see figure on page 69)—often these two formations exist together, a fortunate blend of each crystal's qualities.

Use this stone whenever you need to revitalize yourself or find balance. Here's a meditation you can use.

Spiral Quartz Meditation

First, use bright sunlight to dedicate your Spiral Quartz. After several hours of sunlight, hold the stone in your projective hand and visualize whatever works best for you when increasing energy—some people like to dance, while others imagine rays of light flowing through their bodies. I like to imagine spirals of energy rippling through me, up and down my spine. I like to hold it while in tree pose during yoga.

Sprouting

Sprouting Quartz

Sprouting Points have a layer or coating of tiny points that appear to be "sprouting" or growing along the base and up the sides of a crystal point; sometimes they only appear on the point—this is commonly seen in Scepter Crystals. The name comes from the German term Sprossenquarz, which means "sprouting quartz," as coined by a German geologist in the 1970s.

There are many varieties of this formation, so it can be one of the most confusing to identify. Sometimes these crystal formations are classified as a type of Elestial; however, what keeps them from being a true Elestial is that an Elestial has multiple, distinct crystal points and faces—the Sprouting Crystal is either one point with a layer of small, flat shapes growing parallel on its sides, or a crystal that seems to sprout upward with many points around it like layers of an artichoke. Sometimes there is one clearly identifiable center crystal point; other times there are many points of similar size.

Sometimes the sprouting effect is quite small, such as a surface that looks like tiny scales. The Scepter Point I have displays these markings on the tip. It almost looks like tiny triangles clustered together.

Yet another variety, referred to as the "candle," has scaly growth along the sides that looks like melted wax. Sometimes the Spirit or Fairy Quartz Crystals are put in this category, but they are quite different. (See Spirit Quartz.)

Use Sprouting Quartz for anything that you wish to grow in strength or increase in abundance. Just like the name suggests, this characteristic symbolizes sprouting of something—tangible or intangible—ideas, feelings, wealth, etc.

Sprouting Quartz Affirmation

Visualize what you wish to increase—wealth, happiness, love, family, energy, even a project or your garden.

CHANT:

Sprout, grow, thrive—
increase, endure, survive.

Spirit

Spirit Quartz

This formation goes by a variety of other names—Cactus Quartz is a common description. What differentiates these from the Sprouting Quartz is that in this stone there is one main center point and that point seems to be encased in a crust of tiny points that, instead of sprouting upward along with the center, shoot outward in a variety of directions—like cactus needles. The points are tiny, producing a glittering effect. The base stone of the Spirit Crystal is so densely covered with tiny crystals that the sides are not visible. This formation is mainly found in South Africa and is most often seen in amethyst, although it can occur in other types of quartz as well.

A type of Spirit Quartz called Fairy Quartz is typically opaque or milky quartz that is covered with a crust of crystals that are much finer—it looks like the crystal was rolled in sugar. This type retains much more of the classic crystal shape—you can typically see all six facets.

Spirit Quartz is a very uplifting and optimistic stone. It can raise hopes and encourage a cheerful attitude. It has a harmonious energy and can be used to clear the aura and align the chakras. It can help one attain a peaceful state during meditation, release fears, and find an overall sense of joy, happiness, and appreciation of the beauty of one's surroundings. Additional properties of the type of stone also apply (amethyst, citrine, smoky, aqua aura, and milky quartz).

Like quartz clusters, Spirit Quartz can enhance and bring harmony and cooperation to social or community experiences, home and family, etc. It can also be used to cleanse other stones and amplify their energy.

Fairy Quartz has the added benefit of boosting the energy of the physical body and is often used by crystal healers. It can be used for fertility and abundance spells as well.

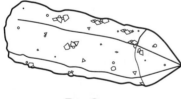

Fairy Quartz

Lift Your Spirits Meditation

You know those bad days we all have sometimes, the ones where you just want to curl up in a ball and cover your head with a blanket? We've all been there. Whatever the reason, we all have days that just don't go as we planned—either we feel inadequate, we've made some kind of blunder, or things just didn't go as we expected. This is inevitable—our reaction, though, can be managed so days like this don't get us down. We are responsible for how we handle setbacks and bad days, but cheering up can be easier said than done. Here's a meditation to help raise your spirits.

If you have an Amethyst Spirit Quartz, see if you can find a candle (or candle holder) in the same shade of violet as your stone. Light the candle and place your Spirit Quartz nearby. I also like to add a couple amethyst points to the arrangement. You can place your candle and crystals in the bathroom while you soak in a relaxing bath or simply set them on a table where you can see them. You can also create an elaborate altar arrangement with flowers and other items that bring you joy (this is also a good altar arrangement to celebrate Ostara—see chapter eight). The idea is to meditate on the sparkle of the crystal in the candlelight and focus on the things that make you happy. What are you grateful for? Put the unpleasant thoughts out of your mind. Lose yourself in the calming energy of the light playing on the crystals. Breathe slowly and deeply. You can also burn incense or listen to your favorite music. Visualize yourself in a place of contentment or imagine the arms of the God and Goddess embracing you—or dancing with you. Use a personal mantra or this chant, if you wish (hold your Spirit Quartz in your receptive hand while you say the words):

> *Love and light wash over me,*
> *lift me up and set me free;*
> *worries will not bring me down,*
> *to fear I am no longer bound;*
> *peace and joy will help me soar,*
> *of self-doubt there is no more.*
> *Now I see a brighter view—*
> *my spirit sparkles fresh and new.*

If your fatigue is rooted in your physical body, use a Fairy Quartz and, as with the previous meditation, use candles and clear quartz points in your arrangement.

CHANT:

Revive, refresh—my body at its best.
Be brave, be strong—my weariness be gone.

Spirit Quartz of other colors may also be used. Just remember they may have a slightly different energy (see the correspondences for that stone in the appendix).

Stacked

This is an unusual and very interesting growth variety. These are not clusters—they are fully developed points that have other fully developed (or nearly fully developed) points either stacked end to end or layered on top of each other. This formation often occurs in Scepter, Tabby, Fenster, and Herkimer Diamonds. Some Stacked crystals consist of one crystal point with multiple terminations. They can technically only be classified as Scepters if the crystals grow in a parallel fashion. Sometimes a fully formed crystal is found growing on the side of another one. They can form what looks like chains of crystals.

Stacked Quartz

Use these as you would any clear quartz point, but think of them as a quartz point multiplied—they pack a punch! They are a multiplication of power. Each crystal adds a boost of energy to the others.

Striated

Look at the sides of your clear quartz points. Chances are you'll see many fine horizontal lines etched across some of them. In fact, half of the clear points I have are striated on at least one side. This formation is actually quite common and part of the natural crystal growth habit. The lines can be on the crystal faces as well as the sides of the base, but this is less common.

Some of these lines are quite deeply etched into the stone—these are the points we'll refer to as Striated. The lines are steplike; you should be able to feel them with your finger. A particular variety called Lemurian Crystals are striated and taper to a point like the Laser Wand Crystal; these are sometimes pale pink or yellow in color.

Striated Crystals are often used in healing and are said to contain ancient knowledge, similar to Record Keepers. Use these points for meditation and to enhance the properties of other stones. Here's a meditation you can use for Striated (and Etched) Crystals.

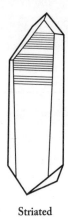

Striated
Quartz

Striated Crystal Meditation

Run your finger or hands across the markings, imagining they are a type of map or code that holds a message for you. Try to let some light shine upon them—sun, moon, or candlelight. If there are markings on several sides of the stone, rotate it in your hands so you can see all the markings. Clear your mind and open yourself to the wisdom of the earth. Imagine knowledge revealed to you, like you're deciphering a secret code.

Tabby

Tabby Quartz Crystals are flattened in appearance—they still retain the classic crystal shape, but they look like someone stepped on them. They are thin and wide—typically twice as wide as they are thick. Tabby Crystals are especially useful in helping you be open to new experiences. They are also good meditation crystals. Tabby Crystals can also be used to activate other stones. Simply place them all in a dish together and charge in sunlight or moonlight.

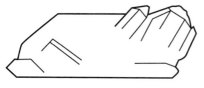

Tabby Quartz

If you're nervous about a new experience that awaits you, or if you're seeking a new opportunity, meditate with the Tabby Crystal.

Tabby Crystal Opportunity Affirmation

I am walking through the gate,
I am stepping through the door.
I will no longer sit and wait—
I am ready to explore.

Trigger

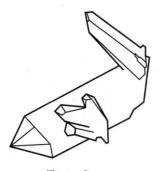

Trigger Quartz

There are two main types of Trigger Crystals. In one type, a smaller crystal point seems to have collided with the main point, often at an angle. Unlike the Bridge Crystal, the point of the smaller crystal in a Trigger is not visible inside the larger point. It seems to have disappeared. Sometimes the trigger point rests against the side of the larger point in a parallel fashion; when the points pressed together are the same size, it's a Twin. In the Trigger, the trigger point is usually considerably smaller than the main crystal.

The other type of Trigger occurs when there is a small point (or points) that seems to be growing out of the main crystal, often at the base, but sometimes it seems to be growing out of the side. In this type, the trigger faces away from the main point instead of facing toward it, and there is a definite point on the Trigger Crystal.

Think of the Trigger as a way to push extra energy through the crystal. You can visualize pushing the trigger to give the crystal a boost. Or, in the case of the points that tilt outward, this is an extra boost to send energy out. In both cases, the energy of the stone is amplified.

For visualization purposes, consider the direction of the triggers. If they go inside, toward the main stone, imagine the energy going into the main crystal before being sent out. If the trigger is pointing outward, imagine energy flowing from all the points—it's more scattered, but still intense.

I have a crystal that's both a Trigger and a Bridge. The main crystal point has a smaller point imbedded in the side in bridge style, and it also has a small trigger point at the base. In this case, a trigger boost of energy for the Bridge Crystal. To gain the full potential from your Trigger Crystal, charge it in direct sunlight.

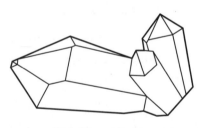

Multi-Trigger Quartz

Multi-Trigger Crystals

We think of clusters as a large mass of crystals—from a dozen to hundreds of points that share a common base. But groups of crystals that consist of only four or five can still be a cluster if they're of uniform size. However, if one of the crystals in the group is larger than the others, you may have a Multi-Trigger Crystal. How can you tell? Check to see if the smaller points are attached directly to the larger one. If they are, it's a Multi-Trigger Crystal. If they simply share a base but are not actually attached to each other, it's a small cluster.

For example, I have a grouping of four quartz points—the largest point has three smaller ones attached to it in a perpendicular style. Picture a quartz point lying on its side and the others sticking up as though they grew out of it. The largest point in this group has a prominent Window; two of the smaller three have Isis points.[1] Generally, I apply the properties of the largest crystal in the group first, followed by secondary properties of the smaller points. In this way, you have an excellent multipurpose crystal. The smaller crystals act as Triggers, adding their particular energy to the other properties of the stone. In this case, I have a Window Crystal with a Trigger boost of Isis energy.

The energy of a Multi-Trigger is different than a cluster. When many crystals are together sharing one base, even if they touch each other and overlap, it's a wide path of energy that can scatter—excellent for entire homes, large rooms, or outdoor spaces. The Trigger Crystal gives you more specific focus since there's one main point with smaller ones to boost the energy. These are ideal for personal use or use between just a few people.

Twin

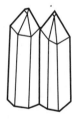

Twin Crystals feature two points that have grown together side by side.

They can be used to facilitate relationships and balance.

The best time to dedicate this crystal is during a first quarter moon, ideally when the moon is in Libra; another favorable time would be during an equinox.

Twin Quartz

---

1 Window and Isis points refer to formations discussed in *The Book of Crystal Spells*. Window Crystals can be used to promote insight and opening the third eye; Isis points have a feminine energy and are used for healing, comfort, fertility, and love.

Twin Crystal Dedication

Place the stone on a surface—table, altar, etc.—and hold both of your palms above the stone, just a few inches away. Visualize your goal and chant twice:

> *Bring us balance, side by side,*
> *two as one we shall abide.*

Carry the stone with you to facilitate the specific relationship for which you dedicated it. When not carrying it, keep it on your altar or in another special place. You may wish to keep it near a photograph of the person with whom you're in a relationship.

Variation: If the other person in the relationship would like to participate with you, each of you should hold one hand above the stone and chant. Keep the stone in a special place or take turns carrying it. This can be a wonderful way to strengthen a relationship. It serves as a symbol that the two of you are putting effort into your bond.

The following crystal descriptions refer to color or inclusions of other minerals rather than shape.

Aqua Aura

Perhaps, like me, you avoid any stones that are artificial or synthetic. I resisted Aqua Aura Quartz for many years because this stone is not found naturally. However, after acquiring it, I changed my mind.

If you've never seen one in person, you'll be impressed. The color is so striking—a very intense bright blue that seems almost otherworldly, which is why I never wanted one—that color *is* unnatural. But these quartz points are not artificially dyed; rather, they are enhanced with a vapor of real gold that is applied at a very high temperature, coating the crystal and bonding with its surface. So, while the process takes place in a lab, the product is still natural and contains no artificial dye. This crystal really is the total package. Since it also possesses the properties of gold, the energy is unique and powerful.

First, Aqua Aura can be used to cleanse the aura and can activate all chakras—especially the throat, third eye, and crown. Additionally, since this stone contains the qualities of gold, it symbolizes purity and nobility—this stone is said to draw knowledge, beauty, success, wealth, and honors into one's life. And it eases responsibility (which undoubtedly one would have after earning all that knowledge, success, and honor!). A "master" healer, according to Melody, it can "release negativity from one's emotional, physical, intellectual, and spiritual bodies". To top it all off, Aqua Aura can help one attune to nature. Whew! That's an amazing stone; I'm glad I have two of them! With all this potential, I couldn't wait to use these crystals.

Aqua Aura "Aura Cleansing"

Since "aura" is in the stone's name, it seems appropriate to use the crystal for an aura cleansing. You can use the crystal with a variety of methods. For example, some people use feathers or smudging to cleanse the aura; others use the combing method or a salt-water bath. With whatever method you use, hold the crystal in your receptive hand to absorb any negativity. When finished, be sure to cleanse the crystal with water and allow it to dry in the sun.

The "I Want It All" Aqua Aura Spell

There's nothing wrong with wanting it all. Success and popularity are craved by many—but most forget about the ability to handle the pressures that can come with it. Some people work too hard for the money and have no time to enjoy life. Some focus too much on success or appearance and suffer from stress or can't seem to find real happiness.

For this spell, think of effortless (and fun) learning experiences, work without stress, a job you love so much it doesn't feel like work, a comfortable material life with plenty of leisure time, and realizing your dreams. Happiness and fulfillment are the real goals. Focus on these qualities as you charge the crystal. You can use one or both of these chants, or write your own. Find a mantra you can repeat easily.

Here's an example:

Wealth, health, and happiness,
I deserve it all.
Brains, beauty, and success,
I deserve it all.

All the dreams I chase,
I handle them with grace.
Foundations that I build,
all my dreams fulfilled.

Place the crystal on your altar or other visible area—be sure you can see it every day—or carry it with you (or wear it). Let it remind you that each day you can take small steps toward your goals. You can have it all, and you deserve it.

Golden Healer

These crystals have a golden-yellow glow that appears to partially or completely cover the crystal surface. This feature is often found in clusters. Actually, the color isn't really on the crystal surface, it's within the stone and occurs during the crystal's growth. The color comes from the presence of another mineral, possibly an iron-hydrate, causing the golden sheen and, sometimes, rainbow effects. These can be used for all healing situations, as well as to promote happiness, success, confidence, and emotional or spiritual healing.

When you need to calm down or be soothed, hold this stone. Visualize its golden tone like a healing light surrounding you and flowing through you, lifting your spirits; yet the presence of iron can have a grounding effect that adds stability. Charge this stone in indirect sunlight.

Herkimer Diamond

Herkimer Diamonds are a special formation of clear quartz first found in Herkimer County, New York. They are characterized by being extremely clear and brilliant, often double-terminated, and short in size. Crystals like this have been found in other places around the world, but true Herkimer Diamonds are only from the Herkimer District. Herkimer Diamonds are not always clear—they can be smoky, golden, or milky—and are not always perfectly shaped.

The specific, unique geological conditions in the area are responsible for these special stones. Scientists believe that fluctuations in temperature, resulting in rapid crystal growth, could play a role. These crystals are usually found in cavities of rock—sometimes hundreds of them are found together! A detailed explanation of the theory can be found at herkimerhistory.com.

The ultimate stone of attunement, this brilliant little crystal can help us recognize and appreciate our true spiritual selves, and our connection with each other and the universe. It facilitates well-being for both people and the earth, and helps us let go of fears so we can relax.

Charge Herkimer Diamonds in bright, direct sunlight. Carry or wear this crystal when you need to feel calm and at peace; meditate with it or sleep with it in your pillowcase. Since these crystals are typically quite small, create a bundle so you can carry it (or several of them) with you. I like to use small drawstring bags.

Lavender Quartz

Lavender Quartz is usually classified as a type of Rose Quartz. It's opaque and pale lavender in color; manganese is thought to be one of the minerals responsible for the hue. Sometimes it's called Lilac Quartz, and it's found mainly in South Africa.

In addition to its qualities of enhancing the third eye (see chapter eight), Lavender Quartz is similar to Rose Quartz, a stone of love, but more intense.

Lavender Quartz Love Spell

Use Lavender Quartz to strengthen a relationship, deepen self-love, or open yourself to new love. This stone has properties similar to Rose Quartz, but stronger. It works faster and with more energy.

Be sure the crystal has been cleansed and charged (water is the best method for cleansing) then rest it on a bed of sea salt. Charge it with both sunlight and full moonlight for a full day. Place the stone next to a pink or white candle and visualize your need.

CHANT:
My heart is open.
Let love I need come to me.
My heart is open.
Let love I have flow through me.
My heart is open.

Lithium Quartz

The presence of the mineral lepidolite is said to be responsible for the lovely violet color of this crystal. Lepidolite contains lithium, thus this crystal's name. It should be easy to distinguish Lithium Quartz from amethyst, especially once you've seen them side by side. Lithium Quartz is not the true purple of amethyst—its shade is a pale pinkish-violet.

Lithium Quartz can help relieve stress, soothe anxiety, and be used with the crown and heart chakras. It's an excellent meditation stone and, like lepidolite, it can help one deal with transitions and change.

Lithium Quartz Affirmation

When you feel anxious about something new in your life—a job, home, or relationship—or if you're feeling stressed and anxious in general, meditate with this stone or carry it with you. Visualize a still pool of water. You are calm. Use this chant:

> *Taking small steps day by day,*
> *I will calmly make my way.*

Tangerine Quartz

This type of quartz is orange in color due to the presence of hematite (iron). When I first encountered these, I was torn between two specimens and was having trouble making a decision (typical Libra)—so I bought both of them. It turns out they're both Record Keepers; oddly enough, I never look for this quality when I'm shopping. I wait until I'm home to examine the pieces closely. Shopping by intuition this way often yields very interesting results!

The rust-orange color is actually a type of staining or coating on the surface of the stone rather than a mineral inclusion. Tangerine Quartz is not to be confused with Fire (or Red) Quartz, which contains hematite and is very dark orange or brownish red. Tangerine Quartz can be used to activate the sacral chakra and is associated with the fire element. Use it in spells for creativity, passion, energy, and strength.

Tangerine Quartz Spell for Strength

Using a platter, plate, or other heat-safe dish, create a display of clear quartz points (and other stones as desired) around an orange, red, or white candle—you may wish to put the candle in an additional container so the wax does not melt onto your crystals. Face the quartz points outward. Hold a Tangerine Quartz Point and visualize sending strength or healing energy to someone (use your projective hand), or to yourself (use your receptive hand), and chant:

> *Mind and spirit, flesh and bone,*
> *strong as iron, like the stone.*

Place the Tangerine Point among the other stones on the platter and allow the candle to burn out. If the strength is for yourself, carry the Tangerine Crystal with you; otherwise, leave it on the altar as long as you like.

Tibetan Quartz

This type of clear quartz point (sometimes appearing smoky) contains inclusions of carbon and/or manganese. They're said to be mined in the Himalayan Mountains, and are often (but not always) double-terminated. They are sometimes referred to as Black Quartz—sometimes they do have a very dark brown, nearly black, appearance. The clearer types often display rainbows, water bubbles, and other inclusions of carbon, manganese, or unidentified minerals that are often dark in color.

Keep in mind that the term "Tibetan" does not necessarily mean the stone is actually from Tibet—these stones could be from other parts of China or throughout the nearby mountains, India, or Pakistan, or even elsewhere in the world. Unfortunately, it's often impossible to be certain exactly where a stone is from, especially since they change hands many times from mining to sales. Also, there are many areas of the world that produce similar stones—laying claim to the name can be hard to prove.

Also remember that sometimes stones will be marketed in a way that makes them sound most appealing—"Tibetan Quartz" sounds exotic and mystical. But even if the crystal is not actually from Tibet, that does not diminish its value.

I have two of these that were marketed as "Tibetan" Quartz and two other specimens that fit this description that were labeled as "quartz with inclusions" from China. They all have a similar appearance and I would classify all these as "Tibetan" or "Black" Quartz.

Tibetan Quartz is said to bring peace and tranquility. According to Melody, they bring "knowledge and information concerning healing and spirituality to the user." If you're engaging in fasting or trying to abstain from something, carry Tibetan Quartz to assist with the process. In addition, it can be used to foster an attitude of acceptance and patience.

Tibetan Quartz Acceptance Affirmation

Ever have a spell that seems to have failed? You may never know why—perhaps in time the true reason will be revealed to you. Other factors you may not be aware of could be at work. Maybe it was "for the good of all" (as we often say) that kept the spell from working as you planned or hoped. We must accept this. We all have dreams and goals we pursue that take time to attain; the only real failure is not trying. Keep taking action toward your goal and don't give up. However, it's easy to say "accept it" and "try again," while it's difficult to overcome the sadness that follows disappointment. Use a Tibetan Quartz Point to meditate on making peace with and accepting a difficult situation.

When the moon is waning or dark, sit in a dimly lit room—candlelight is best—and hold the crystal in your receptive hand. Open yourself to wisdom. (Some say these stones can help you connect with Eastern wisdom—certainly there is much to learn from those cultures. Explore some of those teachings if you wish.) Study the crystal in the candlelight. Then, close your eyes. Chant these words; repeat as desired:

Attachment be released,
clear the way for peace.

– FOUR –

SPECIAL ROCK AND
MINERAL FORMATIONS

Often there are stones I want to explore that simply defy categorization. But, upon taking a closer look, I realized that these stones do, in fact, share a commonality—they are grouped here as "special" because they're an interesting type of rock, a specific blend of minerals, have unusual and noteworthy formations, are found in specific locations, or are formed under specific geologic conditions. In fact, only two of the eleven stones featured here are actually classified as true minerals or crystals.

I selected these stones because I enjoy working with them. Most of them are well-known and easy to obtain, and they have qualities that I believe make them essential for a crystal magic practitioner.

Staurolite: Fairy Cross

Most people interested in the metaphysical properties of stones have heard of or encountered the mineral staurolite, which displays the characteristic twinned crystals that commonly form a "cross" shape. This special shape has made this stone much sought-after by collectors—it has a reputation for being a good luck charm.

Stauros is Greek for "cross"; staurolite is the official state mineral of Georgia—a popular place to find these stones. However, when purchasing, beware of stones that have been ground down or cut—try to find natural formations.

It's somewhat ironic that these stones are called Fairy Crosses—the mineral content is iron aluminum silicate hydroxide; in folklore, fairies are said to detest iron. So, despite their name, they are probably not suited for fairy magic. The properties of iron, however, do suggest strength, so consider these for use as protection amulets.

Fairy Cross Protection Amulet

You can simply carry the stone, but first prepare it by placing it on a bed of salt overnight. Next, pass the stone through incense smoke—frankincense is best. Finally, charge it in sunlight for a couple hours. Fold the stone in an oak leaf, fern frond, or bit of moss. Wrap in a piece of silk or small pouch.

CHANT:
Best of luck and fortune fine,
bring the best to me and mine.

Opal

Opals are not really a "crystal" since they have no ordered structure of atoms—Opal is amorphous (shapeless). Most are volcanic in origin. There is some mystery surrounding the formation of Opals. It's believed they start out as concentrated silica gel that hardens over time in cavities of rock (they often occur in fossils). There are many varieties of Opal—which accounts for its popularity. It's simply one of the most colorful and loveliest gems, and is much sought-after in jewelry. They may dry out or be damaged by heat and light due to the water content, so handle them carefully.

Opal is used to enhance one's characteristics and traits; it strengthens memory, faithfulness, and loyalty. It also helps one "blend" into the background when desired, and can awaken mysticism. Ignore the folklore that says it's bad luck for anyone not born in October (or anyone who's not a Libra) to use this stone. Opal is associated with all the elements so it's a wonderful stone to use in magic.

Opal "Invisibility" Spell

You can use a raw Opal or a piece of Opal jewelry for this spell.

For those moments when you don't wish to be noticed, use this spell to fade into the background. Imagine you are invisible. See the specific situation and visualize that you are unseen. There are many reasons you may want to do this. Perhaps you're not feeling well or you're in a bad mood and simply don't want to be disturbed. We all have days when we'd like to lie low or not be noticed. While it's not healthy to live in seclusion or isolation, this spell can help on those days when you really just need some time to yourself. Hold the stone and chant:

You don't see me, I'm not here,
for this moment, disappear.
Just for now, I am unseen,
veiled, cloaked, behind a screen.

You can end the spell by removing the piece of opal jewelry or by no longer carrying the stone. Be sure to cleanse the stone when you're finished, unless you wish to dedicate it for this specific purpose.

Jade

Jade is another stone that is sometimes classified as a crystal or mineral, but it's more accurately a type of metamorphic rock. Jade typically refers to several different stones, but mainly jadeite and nephrite (a form of actinolite). It often occurs with serpentine—in fact, serpentine is also sometimes sold as Jade. We typically think of Jade as being green, but it can also occur in white, lavender, black, yellow, red, orange, and even blue. The Chinese have famously worked with Jade for at least 4,000 years.

Sometimes referred to as a "dream stone," Jade can be used for remembering dreams and using dreams for problem-solving. A stone of compassion, it can help one to connect with others and become attuned to their needs—it can also help one discern between needs and desires, offering inspiration to pursue what is most important for well-being. And it promotes self-confidence.

Until recently, the only pieces of Jade I had in my collection were a single stone I tumbled in my first rock tumbler and a little carved elephant pendant I've had since childhood, neither of which I could actually confirm as jadeite or nephrite. Even though I finally obtained a piece of nephrite, those pieces of uncertain mineral content still have personal importance for me. Jade is associated with the sign of Libra and, as a Libra, I'm often weighing options—especially needs versus wants. Use this spell to discern desire from true need whenever you're faced with a difficult decision.

Jade Spell for Decision-Making

As with the previous spell using Opal, this spell can be used with a raw or carved piece of Jade or Jade jewelry. If possible, perform this spell during a waxing or full moon in Libra.

Wear or hold the stone while focusing on the decision you need to make.

CHANT:

Help me know, to decide, choice to make, send a sign.

Unakite

Unakite is a combination of three minerals—it's usually classified as a type of granite (epidote granite); sometimes it's called Unakite Jasper. This stone contains pink feldspar, green epidote, and quartz, giving a lovely appearance of shades of green mottled with accents of salmon-pink; the word *epidote* comes from Greek and means "growing together." The name Unakite comes from the area where it was first discovered—the Unakas area of the Great Smoky Mountains. Prized as a semiprecious gemstone, Unakite is commonly carved into beads and cabochons for jewelry.

Metaphysically, Unakite can help you balance mind, body, and spirit. It can be used to remove blockages so you can move forward, love yourself, and release the past. For healing, it's often used in helping one to recover from illness or discover its root cause.

For me, Unakite has been an underappreciated stone. I've had it in my collection for years but I failed to notice its unique qualities. Of course, we all know that stones often come to us when we need them; perhaps that's the reason I didn't pay more attention to it. Someone in my life recently went through a difficult situation and Unakite proved to be of excellent assistance. Here's the spell I used.

Unakite Spell for Balance

Create a simple stretch bracelet of Unakite beads and charge it during a waning moon in Capricorn. This is meant to dispel a cycle that keeps someone trapped spiritually, emotionally, mentally, and/or physically. Use these words to charge the bracelet—it should be worn as long as possible (or you can just use a single stone and carry it). This spell can be performed during a waning moon cycle to release negativity or during a waxing moon to increase strength.

> *Release the past, release the pain,*
> *be happy, healthy—illness wane.*
> *Strength renew, body strong,*
> *overcome the path you're on.*
> *Spirit, mind, and body one—*
> *for good of all, so be it done.*

Picasso Stone

At one of my many visits to local rock and mineral shows, a particular stone caught my eye. It was a gorgeous cabochon pendant set in silver. The stone was gray and black—it looked like someone had painted it to resemble the black silhouette of a bare tree and branches. The vendor told me it was a variety of marble called Picasso Stone—aptly named as it did appear to be painted. It was a work of art by nature's hand. I had to have it.

Research revealed this stone is ruled by Sagittarius, which happens to be my moon sign. And, this is a stone that promotes artistic endeavor—perfect for someone who works in the creative arts. It seems it was meant to be.

In addition to promoting creative talents and artistic endeavors, Picasso Stone also helps one understand his or her destiny and helps transform intuition into clear thought. It fosters strength and perseverance, and helps reduce stress and anxiety.

Here's an affirmation using Picasso Stone for creative inspiration.

Artist's Affirmation

Use this chant to charge a piece of Picasso Stone that you can wear or carry with you. Charge the stone when the moon is in Sagittarius, waxing to full. If you have a current project to focus on, do so. Otherwise, just open yourself to general creativity, inspiration, and fulfilling your artistic dreams.

I have a gift, I have the skill;
my art, my craft, I will fulfill.

Aventurine

This is another stone that is often classified with crystals and minerals but it, too, is actually a rock. It's a type of quartz but is technically not a pure mineral. Sometimes Aventurine is confused with Jade. It's typically green, although it can occur in other shades. The sparkle of Aventurine comes from tiny pieces of other materials in the stone—usually mica or hematite. The mineral fuschite, a type of mica that contains chromium, is the mineral most commonly found in Aventurine and gives it the classic silvery-green color and sparkle. The presence of other minerals can change Aventurine's appearance to brown, orange, or shades of red.

Aventurine is an excellent stone for strengthening your sense of self, achieving tranquility and patience, balancing, and finding adventure. It's also known as a gambler's talisman.

Aventurine Opportunity Spell

This spell is not for creating the opportunity—it's for when the opportunity has arrived and you are competing for it or need to rise to the occasion.

This could be a job interview, a promotion, or any other challenge you face. You can combine Aventurine with citrine and your personal power stone or numerological stone for this spell, if desired. Wear the stone or carry it until the situation has been resolved. Focus and chant:

A time has come, the chance to grow,
the moment's right and this I know.
For this task I am the one,
for good of all let it be done.

Gypsum

Unlike most of the stones in this chapter, Gypsum is a mineral; in fact, it's the most common sulfate mineral. It occurs in such a range of beautiful and unusual formations that I wanted to explore it in detail. Gypsum is known by many additional names—Selenite, Satin Spar, Desert Rose, and Alabaster. This can cause some confusion.

Gypsum forms some of the largest crystals in the world. It can be colorless, white, and shades of red, orange, pink, brown, gray, yellow, and green. If you've ever seen pictures of the famous giant crystal cave in Mexico, with crystals that are nearly 40 feet tall, these are gypsum crystals.

The fibrous form of Gypsum is called Satin Spar due to its pearly, silky appearance—it really looks like satin. This is the type that forms the long wand shapes that resemble stalks of celery. This type is also often cut into smooth shapes that highlight its pearly sheen. In fact, I recently obtained a sphere of orange Satin Spar from Morocco (it was marketed as Selenite). Until now, I've only had clear, white, or pale yellow Gypsum—it's nice to have such a vibrant color in my collection!

Selenite is typically used to refer to the more transparent variety of Gypsum rather than the type with the pearlescent quality; it has transparent crystals in a blade form. Selenite does not contain selenium; it was named for its association with the moon goddess Selene (Greek).

Often the terms Satin Spar and Selenite are used interchangeably or with only subtle differences between the two. One reason for the confusion is that Selenite can sometimes appear somewhat translucent and fibrous, and sometimes it occurs in clear slabs. Generally, if you can see through it, it would be classified as Selenite; if it's translucent or opaque and fibrous with a pearly luster, it's Satin Spar.

The form of Gypsum that occurs in dense, granular masses and is known for its white color is called Alabaster. It has a finer grain than the other forms and has long been carved and used in ornamental work.

Another form, called Desert Rose, is embedded with sand and has an opaque, flowerlike shape. It's also called Sand Rose or Gypsum Rose—not to be confused with the Barite Rose, which is also referred to as Desert Rose. Once you've seen both types of Desert Rose, the difference is clear.

There are some additional, unusual forms of Gypsum. You can even find single or twinned blade-like crystals embedded with sand. Ram's Horn is another interesting formation—it has a curling shape that resembles a horn. There's also Swallowtail Twin or Fishtail Twin—these are V-shaped.

The word *gypsum* comes from the Greek word for "plaster," *gypsos*. It was also called "spear stone" in Old English. It's a fairly soft mineral and very common. Gypsum is noted as an excellent fertilizer; it's also used in drywall and plaster.

Generally, Gypsum can be used to promote fertility and creativity; it's often called a lucky stone and can be used to end stagnation and encourage growth. The Satin Spar variety strengthens mental clarity, judgment, and awareness. Alabaster energizes other minerals and can be used to encourage forgiveness. Selenite can be used to increase material success as related to business ventures; it also aids mediation on past and future lives and helps with decision-making.

Gypsum Rose Motivation Spell

Let's face it—we all have times when we need a kick in the behind to get moving. I feel that way in the winter, when I'm just not in the mood to exercise—I want to do it, but I just can't seem to take that first step. To end those times of stagnation, when you simply feel unmotivated, try this spell.

First, charge the stone(s). Visualize your goal or goals—state your intent out loud. Hold the stone(s) in your projective hand and chant:

Motivate me to succeed,
give encouragement I need.
When I see this special stone,
remind me of the goals I own.

Keep the Gypsum Rose in a place where you will see it—on the kitchen counter, for example, or on the bathroom sink or living room coffee table. The stone is a visible reminder of your goal. If you have several pieces, place one in each room of your home—you can even keep one in the car. You need to see the stone(s) several times each day.

Forgiveness Spell

Whether you need to forgive yourself or someone else, on a new moon night write down your feelings on a piece of paper, fold it, and place a piece of Alabaster on top of it. Place a candle in a container on top as well. If you have a candle holder made of Alabaster, use that. This combines the magic of earth (acceptance, nurturing) and fire (transformation) to help you deal with the issue. Focus on your need as you watch the candle burn. When you're ready, burn the paper and bury the ashes. Cleanse the stone.

Selenite Past or Future Life Meditation

Imagine your clear piece of Selenite Gypsum as a window into a past or future life—open yourself to the experience and lessons you need to learn.

You can meditate with the stone or place it on your nightstand while you sleep (or both). Use this chant if you wish:

Where I've been or where I'll go,
show me what I need to know—
lessons that I need to learn,
issues of the most concern.

Satin Spar Wand Spell for Focus

For this spell, use a wandlike piece of Satin Spar Gypsum. Visualize the wand as an actual magic wand, a symbol of power and creativity. In this case, you are seeking to stimulate your mental clarity and awareness. Hold the stone wand in your receptive hand, imagining it as a channel to receive energy and aid problem-solving.

CHANT:
Focus, sharpen, crystallize—
my thoughts and visions realize—
articulate and organize,
solutions will materialize.

Soapstone (Steatite)

Soapstone is a metamorphic rock. It's comprised mainly of talc, along with varying other minerals. It occurs in shades of brown, gray, green, or white, and is often used in carvings. Sometimes the mineral pyrophyllite is called soapstone, but it lacks the "soapy" feel when touched. The more talc in the stone, the softer it is. You may have items made from soapstone—candle holders or incense and aromatherapy burners. These are quite popular. This stone promotes the widening of one's horizons—compelling one to take action and explore new experiences, as well as face new challenges. Use

Soapstone to help you release old habits and embrace the new. It has a calming, peaceful feeling. For a spell using Soapstone, see chapter two for "The Fool: Opportunity Spell."

Anyolite (Ruby in Zoisite)

Zoisite is a mineral (Tanzanite is the most popular form), but when it's found in a special combination with ruby and black hornblende, it's referred to as Anyolite. Like Soapstone, this is a metamorphic rock. And it's a lovely stone—a beautiful combination of magenta (ruby) and emerald green (chrome zoisite) with sparkling accents of black and darker green (due to the mineral tschermakite—black hornblende). The name comes from the Maasai word for green: *anyoli*. It's found mainly in Kenya and Tanzania.

This pairing of minerals makes for a special, magical energy. Zoisite is excellent for dispelling negativity and uplifting one's energy; ruby amplifies energy and stimulates the intellect, and enhances spiritual wisdom; hornblende helps one recognize duality, increases creativity, stimulates mental processes, aids meditation, and promotes understanding and acceptance. It has also been said to foster communication with animal spirit guides. In addition to all these properties, as the combined mineral Anyolite, this stone can help the user reach altered states of consciousness and helps one tap into his or her abilities and talents. Psychic abilities can also be amplified with this stone. According to Melody, Anyolite "increases the awareness of one's individuality while allowing one to maintain connectedness with humanity."

Tap into Your Talents Spell
Use this spell to access your untapped potential or to further enhance your current talents. Charge a piece of Anyolite (or a piece set as jewelry). Visualize your need and chant:

Undiscovered talents I possess,
be revealed to me when time is right.
Guide all my endeavors to express
and discover ways to share and to delight.

Septarian Nodule

The Septarian Nodule is a type of concretion. Some sources even categorize it as a geode; it is kind of like a fossilized, cracked ball of mud. The nodule referred to here is a beautiful, round, brownish-gray rock (limestone) that looks like it has been cracked—there are darker brown veins (aragonite) that seem to outline golden-yellow crystallized areas (calcite). Sometimes pyrite or other minerals are present.

This type of formation can be found throughout the world, but this specific type is from an area of the U.S. that is now southern Utah. The exact process of their formation is a bit mysterious but, basically, during the Cretaceous Period, approximately 50–70 million years ago, sediment from the retreating Gulf of Mexico was left to dry and crack; calcite from the shells of sea animals decomposed, then seeped into the clay and became crystallized—some of the calcite formed into aragonite and separated the calcite from the clay.

Since these nodules contain cracks or cavities, the name Septarian came to be used when describing them (septaria). The name comes from the Latin word *sept* or *septum*, which means "partition" (precinct means *septa*) referring to the dividing cracks (not in reference to the crack splitting into seven, which would be *septem*; this is a common error).

The spherical nodule shape makes these excellent touchstones, but they can be found in rough slabs and other shapes as well. Metaphysically, these stones combine the properties of calcite and aragonite. Calcite amplifies energy, aids with the study of the arts and sciences, and promotes awareness and appreciation of one's surroundings; aragonite aids in centering, meditation, insight, patience, and responsibility. This stone is excellent for stimulating the root and solar plexus chakras.

Acceptance Affirmation

When dealing with a stressful situation you can't avoid, meditate using a Septarian Nodule. Visualize handling the issue with strength and ease.

> CHANT:
> *I am patient, I accept, there are things I can't neglect.*
> *Give me strength and give me grace to handle everything I face.*

Shiva Lingam Stone

These rocks are a type of cryptocrystalline quartz (meaning the crystals are too small to see with the naked eye) with deposits of iron-oxide. They are gray and brown to reddish brown, often with patterns or lines, and shaped like a long, narrow egg.

Lingam or *linga* (Sanskrit) means "mark" or "sign," but the word has many other meanings and uses. In this context, these stones can be said to symbolize the energy of the Hindu god Shiva. This, however, is a deceptively simplistic definition. The origin of this symbol can be found in the description of the first Shiva-linga, a kind of cosmic pillar, an oval-shaped stone that represents the entire universe. Stones of this type that are naturally formed are held to be sacred. However, manmade versions of these stones can be purchased and are said to represent the union of male-female energies—knowledge and wisdom.

According to Tsa-Jon Narain, an Indo-Tibetan art dealer and Indologist who deals in these stones, in an article from *Hinduism Today*, there are "classic tantric" markings consisting of a horizontal line around the middle of the stone, ideally three-quarters from the bottom—this symbolizes the elevation of consciousness. The stone should be placed upright; this is to represent the third eye. The classic Lingam should be smooth, gray in color with markings in red, "not too fat, not too thin," and polished to a shine.

Found in the Narmada River in India, a place considered to be sacred, the stones are gathered once a year (during the dry season), selected carefully for the best markings, and hand-polished. Certainly it would be remarkable to find a natural one, but these hand-polished ones are still extremely special. Don't worry if your stone doesn't have the classic markings described here.

Shiva Lingam stones are also used to represent the origin of all things, the cosmic egg of creation—Shiva is known as both the creator and destroyer. The stones can be used for balancing, to symbolize earth energy, to aid meditation, and to awaken Kundalini. They are often used in Buddhism as well.

Shiva Lingam Dedication Ritual

To dedicate your Shiva Lingam stone, arrange your altar as desired, mark the four quarters, light candles, and decorate with a variety of plants and flowers. Place your stone in the center of the altar and meditate on its symbolism.

Use this stone as a reminder of the magnificence of the universe and respect for life. It can be a valuable centering and meditation stone, raising awareness of our connection to all things.

CHANT:
Universal energy,
power to destroy and to create—
I am awake.
Origin of all things,
mystery of life that rules us all—
I am in awe.

Great Spirit,
elements of fire, water, earth, and air—
I am aware.

Dalmatian Stone

Sometimes called Dalmatian Jasper or Polka Dot Jasper (or even Dalmatian Agate), the Dalmatian Stone is actually an igneous rock; however, it's a very interesting rock—a blend of quartz and the minerals albite (a type of feldspar) and arfvedsonite (named for a Swedish chemist). It's often dyed bright colors. In its original state, it looks like the coat of a Dalmatian—white or grayish white with black spots.

This is a good initiation stone—it can be used to awaken a childlike wonder and sense of joy. It can increase cheerfulness in one's environment; it can also help one understand and release painful experiences. The presence of arfvedsonite allows for manifestation of a goal—it clears the path; albite provides clarity, certainty, and cooperation. Dalmatian Stone has been noted as a good stone for children and pets and, due to its name, it's reputed to be especially good for working with dogs.

Pet Healing Spell

In addition to the Dalmatian Stone you will need:

- a candle (white or brown) and candle holder
- a tiny clipping of your pet's fur or a whisker (or another part that's naturally shed)
- a pinch of cinnamon
- a garnet (optional)

Place the whisker, hair clipping, etc. under the candle holder. Sprinkle a dash of cinnamon in the holder and insert the candle. Place the stone (or stones) next to the candle holder, visualize your need, and light the candle. Say whatever words you wish; let the candle burn out.

Hag Stones

You may already be familiar with the lore that says a stone with a hole worn through it is good luck. I remember hearing that from my grandma when I was a child. Folklore is filled with uses for these rocks—holey stones, holed stones, or hag stones are all terms that refer to rocks with natural holes worn through them. They've also been called witch stones and even goddess stones; there are many tales of these special stones being used for protection and good luck.

The name Hag Stone has origins in folk magic beliefs—the stones were worn, carried, or hung in homes and barns to keep evil hags from causing harm. Excusing the stereotype of witches as hags, these stones can be used to repel negative energy. There's a legend about evil hags who would enter a person's bedroom at night and sit on the victim's chest—this is also related to vampire folklore and was said to be a source of nightmares. Hag Stones were hung on bedposts to protect the sleeper as well as dispel nightmares. These stones were also said to be built into the walls of homes for protection; fishermen used them, too. They were nailed to doors of homes and barns, and hung above thresholds and windows. Another folk magic belief is that looking through the hole in a stone would enable a person to see fairies.

A legend of St. George found in an ancient English manuscript dated between 1420–1450 gives specific instructions for using a holed stone for protecting horses. It was said that if a horse appeared tired in the morning, an evil witch or fairy had been riding it during the night; hanging a piece of holed flint in the stable was said to protect from this. The stone should be hung at the stable door or over the horse's stall with a verse to St. George.

Tales of holey stones appear in the myths and legends of a variety of cultures. In a Welsh version of the Percival story, the hero is able to see and kill a monster by looking through a magic stone. A very specific type of holey stone referred to as adder stones, serpent's eggs, or Druid's glass is said to be magical and also has the ability cure snakebites. Wishing stone is yet another term used. They have also been used to promote fertility and easy childbirth.

Beyond the fact that these stones share a common appearance—they contain holes—there are other ways to distinguish them. Some of these stones are water-worn and smooth, while others are lumpy and cavernous, displaying rough ridges and valleys. There's a reason for these distinct appearances. Various types of weathering can cause holes in stone— organic weathering is a general term for rock worn away by water, roots of plants, acids from lichens, animals, and erosion by other rocks and minerals. Abrasion from ice or forced fracturing from chemical reactions can also cause holes to form. Finally, stress or pressure and rapid temperature changes can form holey stones as well. Pits and depressions in stone caused by animals such as mollusks can even form holes.

We can also use numerology (see chapter 5) to determine how to use these stones. Count the number of holes and choose a purpose based on the corresponding number. Examine the stone carefully, looking for places where light shines through. Some holes do not penetrate all the way through the stone; others are curved and twisted. You may need to use a magnifying glass to find all the holes. For a stone that's extremely porous, don't worry about trying to count all the openings; use it for another purpose that doesn't depend on numerology.

Often the unique shape of these stones can appear in forms that look like faces or skulls. If you see a shape in the stone, use it as the symbol it represents. Some Hag Stones will also contain crystals.

As with many things in nature that are rare, one is considered lucky to come across a Hag Stone. You can often find them near streams and rivers, but sometimes you will find them in places where the water is long gone. If you don't have access to a place where you can find these, you may be able to purchase them from other rock enthusiasts in stores, online, or at gem and mineral shows.

I like to keep these stones outside where they can be exposed to a variety of weather conditions. If you have a large collection of these stones, use them to create a circle for spell-casting, or just use four of them to represent the quarters. If you just have one Hag Stone, it can be used to represent the earth element on your altar.

Hag Stone Protection Spell

During a waxing moon phase, or on a full moon night, place your stone (or stones) near one or more thresholds and windows. You can put the stones in visible places or hide them in planter boxes or hanging baskets. If you wish, hang small ones from a cord and display them in windows or set them on the window sill. Whatever method you choose, visualize your space being protected inside and out. Use this chant as you place your stone(s):

> *Hag Stone, keep ill will at bay,*
> *drive all trespassers away.*
> *Guard this place all night and day.*

To Banish Nightmares

On a waning moon night, place a Hag Stone in your bedroom either under your bed or by hanging it from a cord on your bedpost. Visualize a peaceful night's rest undisturbed by nightmares. Picture the nightmare as a shadow hovering in the room and being sucked into the holes in the stone. The nightmare is not just trapped, it is destroyed, dissolved. Use this chant to seal the spell:

Holey stone, protect my sleep,
nightmares drawn into your keep.

Good Luck Charm

Carry a small Hag Stone with you for good luck. You can simply keep it in your pocket or purse. You can even wear one, if you have one that is suitable for stringing on a chain or ribbon. Charge it first by allowing it to sit outside for a few days. Try to expose it to moonlight, sunlight, wind, and rain (or snow). Next, visualize good fortune coming your way—see yourself being lucky in everything you do. Here's a chant to help you:

No matter what the day may bring,
sun or clouds, wind or rain,
fortune's face will smile on me,
grant me luck in everything.

Hag Stone Garden Spell

If you have a garden, use Hag Stones to enhance it (along with other crystals). If you don't have one, you can still use Hag Stones outside to add a magical touch to plants and outdoor spaces (you can use them on a patio or balcony, too, if you don't have a yard). As you place the stone(s), chant *tutum hortus*. In Latin, this means "safe garden."

– FIVE –

QUARTZ CRYSTAL
POINT GRIDS

The Book of Crystal Spells explored a variety of grid shapes and stone combinations, following detailed patterns, using many different stones. The grids here, while they may seem simpler, are no less powerful. These grids are patterns that use only (or mainly) clear quartz points. However, you can always substitute other crystal points as needed, depending on your goal.

Crystal points can act as tiny wands, focusing and directing our energy. Utilizing various shapes and numerological correspondences, grids can be created for just about any magical need. These grids are mainly based on numerology—they are arranged by the number of points used and the correspondences of those numbers. In addition, direction of the points can be used for drawing energy toward something or sending it out.

Planning a Grid

Using crystal points, you can create endless patterns of shapes and lines. One way to keep the flow of energy smooth is to be sure all the points are facing a uniform direction. The position of the stones depends on your intent. When creating a shape like a circle or square, face the crystal points in a clockwise direction to draw things to you; arrange them counterclockwise to dispel something. Ideally, the crystals should touch each other; however, when creating a large grid, you can leave small spaces between the stones.

When you construct a grid shape that has right angles, you can use "corner" stones to assist with the flow of energy. If you imagine energy flowing from the tip of a point, but you have a right angle, that energy could just keep going. Instead, you want something to catch it and direct it into the next stone, so the energy can "turn" the corner. Other shapes, such as straight lines, don't need these extra stones, but you can use them to "flavor" the energy you are directing. For example, you can use amethyst or rose quartz corner stones in a clear quartz grid. They will add a more specific intent to your goal. Of course, you can just use bits of clear or milky quartz, if you wish.

Refer to chapter three for special quartz points you can also incorporate into your grids.

Basic Numerological Associations

- **2** = harmony of opposites; unity
- **3** = expansion, good fortune, spiritual trinities
- **4** = stability
- **5** = health, life force
- **6** = love, harmony
- **7** = wisdom, spirituality

- **8** = strength, power, material success
- **9** = change and inspiration
- **10** = balance and completeness

Candle Grids

Positioning crystal points in a circle, points facing toward a candle, helps you charge a candle with energy before lighting it for use in a spell. Visualize the energy of the stones sending energy to the candle.

Another candle grid style is to arrange the crystals with points facing outward, the bases of the stones touching the candle. You can think of the grid as similar to a magic circle you cast for rituals or spellwork, but on a smaller scale. Visualize the energy of the candle being amplified by the crystals and sent out with your intent.

Grids for Balance and Relationships

A pair of stones can create a sense of balance, especially in situations concerning relationships or a union of opposites. There are several ways to arrange these points, depending on your goal. Place them parallel to each other to direct double force toward a goal. Two people working together can use this method to unite their energies.

Grids (for balance and relationships)

To create a face-to-face exchange, sit across from someone and place two stones on the table, parallel to each other. Each of you should have a point facing you. The alternative is to use double-terminated points.

For yet another version, place a crystal or cluster in the center, or a candle, and visualize a ball of energy in the center, flowing through the stones toward each of you.

Maiden Mother Crone Grid

This grid uses three crystals to symbolize the trinity of Maiden, Mother, and Crone. If you have them, use three different crystal points—use amethyst for the Maiden, clear quartz for the Mother, and smoky quartz for the Crone. If you don't have these types of crystals, just use all clear quartz.

Maiden
Mother
Crone Grid

Place the amethyst point at the bottom of the triangle, point facing left. Next, add the clear quartz on the left side, pointing toward the top; finally, place the smoky point on the right, facing down toward the bottom. Use corner stones if you wish. This symbolizes a flow of energy from youth to maturity, then middle age to old age, in a cycle, flowing in a clockwise direction.

When you place the three stones, use the following words:

Maiden: *As the moon controls the tides, so its rhythm rules our lives.*

Mother: *Through cycles changing, wax and wane, in different phases, yet the same.*

Crone: *We journey—Maiden, Mother, Crone, in strength together and alone.*

Repeat three times to raise energy: *Maiden, Mother, Crone—together and alone.*

This layout can be used to celebrate a rite of passage or honor a change, life stage (puberty, pregnancy, birth, wedding, or menopause), or simply to acknowledge the cycles of life. This grid can be used in a group by designating a person to represent each stage. That person places the crystal and speaks the corresponding words, then everyone chants the final lines together.

The Pinnacle Grid

This grid uses three stones in an inverted V-shape. Think of this one as reaching a pinnacle or summit of a mountain. You can concentrate and focus energy this way by pointing two crystals upward and, where their points meet, position the third stone at the top.

You can also use this arrangement for the Maiden Mother Crone Grid, placing whichever stone you wish to focus on at the top—the other two represent support.

The Pinnacle is an excellent way to focus and direct energy—try using this with a candle. You can make a larger version by placing a Pinnacle arrangement on four sides of a candle, a Pinnacle pointing in each direction.

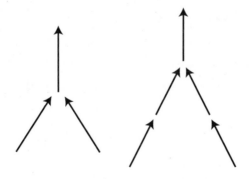

Pinnacle Grids (3 vs. 5 crystals)

You can also make a Pinnacle with five crystals, placing one point at the top and two on each side below it.

Cross Grid

The most balanced four-point grid is a simple cross; four is a number of stability. You can face the points outward or inward. Simply arrange them like points on a compass. These are useful for marking the quarters or representing the four elements. If you want to charge an object, place the item in the center of the cross with the crystal points facing inward.

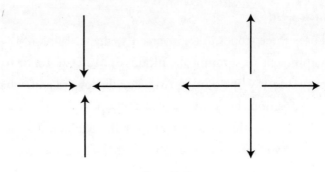

Cross Grids

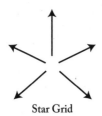

Star Grid

Star Grid for Health

Five is the number for health and the life force. The best way to create a grid with five crystals is to make a simple star shape. Put the largest crystal at the top, then one on each side facing outward, and the other two pointing downward. Put the base of the crystals in the center so the points radiate outward. Again, you may put a candle or other object in the center—a Golden Healer Crystal is a good choice. Use this grid to send out healing energy. Chant as you place each of the five points—lower left, lower right, upper left, upper right, top:

By the strength of five,
energy to heal—

Energy to thrive—
now hear my appeal.
Health shall be revived.

An alternative method is to have all the points facing inward to charge an object.

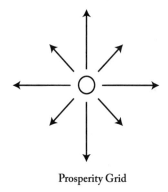

Prosperity Grid

Prosperity Grid

This is a very simple, yet powerful, grid for prosperity. You will need eight clear quartz points and a piece of Tiger Eye for the center. Place the quartz points facing outward. Use your four largest points to create a cross and then fill in the spaces between them with the four smaller ones, pointing out diagonally. Move in a clockwise direction.

As you position the piece of Tiger Eye, say:

I deserve all the abundance the universe has to offer.

Visualize your needs. As you work your way around clockwise, beginning at any point on the grid, say these words as you place each crystal—you will say the entire chant twice:

I am open to receive,
I deserve and I believe.
Let abundance come to me,
for good of all so shall it be.

The Feather Grid

Using nine points—one very large and eight smaller ones—you can create a grid I like to call the "feather." Since one of the numerological uses for the number nine is inspiration and feathers are often associated with that as well, I like to use this grid for increasing creativity.

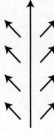

Imagine the longest crystal is the center spine of the feather and the others radiate outward and upward alongside it, smaller ones at the top, moving to larger ones toward the bottom. This works best if your largest point is long and narrow. This design is excellent for sending energy outward—especially for creative works you plant to share with others.

Feather Grid

Place the center crystal first, then start at the bottom right, moving back and forth until the grid is complete. Speak a line of the chant as you place each stone:

I tap into the source,
I am starting strong,
I will not give up,
I will stay on course.
I will move along
at a steady pace;
my goal is now in sight—
I will win the race.
I can now take flight.

The Sprout Grid

Use nine crystal points to visualize a project starting small and increasing. If you have some Sprouted Quartz Points, use them as part of this grid.

Start at the bottom and lay out the three center stones. Then fill in the remaining six by starting with the bottom four, then adding the upper two. When the grid is complete, visualize your goal and chant:

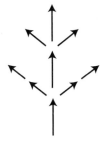

What I nurture, what I tend,
let it increase and transcend—
progress now will take effect.
Rise above what I expect.

Grid for Completion

For this grid, you will create a design that looks like a figure 8. It's a well-balanced grid, six pieces on each side.

Sprout Grid

Start in the center and work your way around, up, and over (clockwise) then down (counterclockwise) and back to the center.

The number twelve represents completeness. Use this grid if you're feeling unsatisfied, incomplete, or unfinished—or if you have some aspect of your life that feels this way. Meditate on your situation to seek a solution.

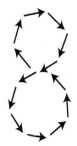

CHANT:
Something's missing, not quite whole,
find what's needed—search my soul.

Circles and Starbursts

Circles are one of the most natural grids to create. You can always put a large crystal in the center—a generator point would be the best choice—and build layers of outward-facing

Completion
Grid

points in a circle. This is excellent for group rituals, too. You can also stagger the points for a starburst effect.

Starburst Grid

More Grid Information

While size doesn't matter when considering crystal "power," size can play a role in your grids. Whenever possible, try to use stones of a uniform size. If you do have one or two that are considerably larger than the others, place those stones parallel at the top or bottom of a grid to create a balanced energy.

You can also use other types of quartz points, such as amethyst, smoky quartz, or citrine, if they correspond to your specific goal. But remember they will change the influence of your spell, adding a subtle difference to the energy. Think of it like spices in food: sometimes you want complexity, and sometimes salt is the only seasoning you need. Adding one different type of quartz point to a grid, at the top of a triangle, perhaps, can be a nice touch. Balance is the key. If you want to use two amethyst points in your grid, for example, position them parallel to each other.

Experiment by creating your own grids—try the various shapes here or create spirals and curves. Consult the numerology chart in the appendix for more ideas. You may wish to photograph them or make sketches of grids you create so you can remember your designs. Grids can be left in place for as long as you like—trust your instincts. Just remember that if you think you may need to move it, create it on a tray, platter, or piece of wood or sturdy cardboard.

– SIX –

CHALCEDONY GROUP

I decided to create a chapter specifically for this category of stones since there is such an interesting variety of this type. In fact, some mineral sources even disagree on the definition of chalcedony—sometimes this term is used for only the blue and white forms and excludes agates and jaspers. For our purposes here, we'll use the most common definition, which does include agates and jaspers. And since these stones are often confused with one another due to similarities in appearance, they deserve some special attention.

Quartz is divided into two main families: crystalline (forming distinct crystals) and cryptocrystalline. The cryptocrystalline (sometimes called microcrystalline) group contains stones with atoms packed tightly; they are fibrous in appearance rather than forming crystals, and they have a mostly opaque or translucent appearance. These stones contain crystals that are so small you need a microscope to see them. Since these stones are translucent and almost never transparent, they are not used as faceted stones.

However, these stones have been carved into decorative shapes, cabochons, vases, statues, and jewelry for thousands of years. This is commonly known as the chalcedony group.

Before we begin, I'd like to address what some may consider omissions from this group. Some sources include Aventurine in this group; however, most of my research classifies it as technically a rock, so it's explored in chapter four. Sometimes Tiger Eye is also found in this category. However, since Tiger Eye is generally thought to be a pseudomorph mineral (or, more recently, a synchronous mineral growth and not a replacement) I have not included it here. Onyx is part of this category, but since I explored that stone in detail in my previous book, I will not repeat that discussion. And now, on to our main event—the agates and jaspers (and a few other noteworthy stones).

Agate is one of the most abundant stones on earth. Its name derives from the Achates River in Sicily, where it was first discovered thousands of years ago. Often banded, translucent, or nearly opaque, it occurs naturally in a variety of colors and patterns. Some agates have very distinctive designs and are given special names, such as Moss Agate and Blue Lace Agate. The bands of agate often contain dramatic curves and shapes; bands of Onyx have a more parallel design. However, there are some agates that lack the banded pattern. There is rich folklore surrounding the use of agate—placed in the mouth it was said to quench thirst; placed on the forehead it was said to cure fever. Another legend says if someone wears an agate, that person cannot tell a lie. In addition, agate has been carved into a variety of shapes—statues, bowls, etc.—throughout the ages. Agates like "crazy lace" and "eye" agates display gorgeous banding and circle patterns. However, agate is easily dyed and most of the very brightly colored ones being sold are artificially colored. There are some spectacularly colored natural ones, though, in shades of orange, brown, yellow, and even pale pink.

Jasper is a rock that consists of 80% microcrystalline quartz, and tends to be opaque. In addition, sometimes jaspers contain other types of chalcedony. These stones have also been used to create jewelry and other decorative items and have been prized throughout history for their use in magic and healing. Technically, the stone we call jasper is a form of chert (flint is a type of chert and chert contains quartz) and it usually occurs in red (presence of iron causes the reddish color), yellow, brown, and sometimes green—often a blending of colors. While jasper can be striped or banded, mottled or blotched, like agate it's often characterized by specific patterns—there are "picture" jaspers that resemble landscape scenes, and a variety called "leopard skin" that looks like the spotted coat of a leopard. Jaspers are also sometimes named for the location where they're found. The name jasper means "spotted or speckled stone."

How can you tell the difference between agate and jasper? One way is by how much light passes through the stone. A transparent stone is one you can see through; a translucent stone lets some light through; an opaque stone allows no light to pass through. Agate is translucent to semi-transparent; some are banded, some have mossy inclusions or other designs, and some have no markings at all. Jasper is mainly opaque; it contains more impurities than agate. The problem is that it can be tricky to tell if a stone is actually semi-translucent or truly opaque because some stones have areas that span the range between both.

Another area of confusion is determining of what minerals the stone is made. For example, rhyolite, a type of rock, is sometimes sold under the name jasper. In fact, many jaspers can also be categorized as rocks since they can be made of more than one mineral. When shopping for stones, be aware of some of these slight variations in name.

Now, let's explore some of these beautiful stones!

General Properties

- *Chalcedony:* Excellent stone for balancing body and mind with emotions and spiritual pursuits. A stone of "brotherhood" that can remove melancholy and enhance generosity.

- *Agate:* A very balancing stone; good for stabilizing the aura. Can aid cleansing and removal of negativity. Useful for self-examination and general well-being, and can also be used to increase perception and to stimulate one's innate talents and capabilities.

- *Jasper:* Often referred to as the "supreme nurturer." Can help one find comfort and peace in isolation while knowing you're not truly alone. A shaman's stone; use to stimulate the solar plexus chakra; balancing and grounding; dispels negativity; stabilizes the aura; aids astral travel; can help stabilize one's energy. Jasper has also been called "the rain bringer" as it was believed to bring rain in times of drought and keep ships safe during storms.

Agate Spells

Tree, Moss, and Dendritic Agates

There is often some confusion surrounding these types of agates, so let's look more closely at these three stones.

Tree Agate gets its distinct markings from the varying presence of chlorite, manganese, or hornblende. The markings often have the appearance of treelike shapes. When the shapes take on a very distinct tree shape, they have earned the name Dendritic, which comes from the Greek word for tree—*dendron*. Tree Agate is usually the opaque, white-colored stone with green-colored inclusions; Moss Agate is generally the translucent type displaying lots of green "mossy" inclusions—like looking at algae in a pond; Dendritic can be either type—usually with the most distinct tree or fernlike shapes. Sometimes the names Tree and Moss Agate are used interchangeably. Differentiating between these two can be daunting, but they're such similar stones that it probably won't matter if you mix them up.

Here are some subtle distinctions in the use of these agates:

- Dendritic Agate is a stone of gentleness; can help one center and be present in the moment. Useful to connect with the plant kingdom, encourage Earth-healing, and to increase abundance. Calming and soothing.

- Moss Agate enhances agreeability and persuasiveness; can improve one's self-esteem. Balances emotions, brings out the best in one's personality, and aids communication and connection with the plant and mineral kingdoms. It increases abundance and helps you see the beauty all around you. Excellent for Earth-healing.

- Tree Agate promotes peace and meditation, abundance, and connection to nature.

Ritual for Connecting with Nature

As you decorate your altar or other sacred space, think "Nature"—capital N. Use anything that represents nature to you—including live plants, leaves, flowers (fresh or dried) and herbs, pine cones, shells, feathers, moss—create a shrine dedicated to Mother Earth. The goal of this spell is to reconnect with nature on a personal level. Of course, it's ideal if you can actually get outside for the ritual—use a tree stump or large rock as a simple altar (nature provides all the decoration you need).

Use any combination of Tree, Moss, or Dendritic Agate in tumbled or raw form, or even a piece of jewelry. You will be dedicating this piece (or pieces) to keep the essence of nature with you at all times, reminding you of your connection with the earth and the sacredness of all life on the planet. The result will be a calming, soothing stone that not only brings the solitude of nature to you wherever you are, but will help you keep an Earth-conscious attitude.

Hold your stone(s) or piece of jewelry in your projective hand. First you will project the desired energy into the stone; later you should hold it in your receptive hand to receive the energy and utilize it or, if it's a necklace, just wear it. (Wear a ring or bracelet on your receptive hand.)

Using your altar, or the natural world around you, visualize connecting with the earth. This visualization will vary with each individual—only you know what works best for you. Some people may be drawn to the sea, others to the mountains. If you can't be in your favorite place, visualize it. Or simply focus on the images on your altar or the nature around you. If you only have access to a public park, focus on the trees—or even a single leaf or acorn. If you can't immerse yourself in your desired place, create it using a combination of visualization and props—again, use items on your altar, even photos. Play recordings of nature sounds or use a fountain.

Once you have visualized your ideal place (or state of mind) in nature, imagine what you see, feel, and hear being preserved inside the stone. Gaze upon the stone and see nature unfolding within it. Know that no matter where you are, you can feel this connection any time you hold or wear the stone. It will remind you of Mother Earth and the need to care for her; it will also help you seek the peaceful state of mind you establish now.

Here's a chant that can help you complete the ritual:

Sacred earth and sacred stone,
Mother Nature, this is home.

My dedication strong and true,
we are all a part of you.

If you created an altar you can leave in place for awhile, let your stone rest there for a few days.

Blue Lace Agate Affirmation

Blue Lace Agate is a popular stone for its beautiful bands of pale blue and white. It's especially good for the throat chakra (can also be used with heart, third eye, and crown). It's best known for its use in aiding spiritual pursuits and self-exploration. For this spell, use the stone as a symbol on your spiritual journey to learn to live in the moment and release any pain and worry from the past. Each day is a new beginning; each night, embrace your sleep as a reset button as you prepare for a new day in the morning.

Place a piece of Blue Lace Agate in a location where you will see it every day, ideally in the morning. One really good location is your bedroom nightstand—you will see it when you wake up and just before you go to sleep. When you see the stone, use the following affirmations (or write your own) to give yourself a restart every day. You may hold the stone while you chant, if you wish.

MORNING AFFIRMATION:
Day is new.
From rest I awaken feeling blessed.
Day is new.
Free from the past, I am refreshed.
Day is new.

BEDTIME AFFIRMATION:
Day is done.
I prepare to rest, feeling blessed.
Day is done.
Today becomes the past; it doesn't last.
Day is done.

Turritella Agate Spell to Release Worry

Turritella Agate occurs in beautiful shades of brown containing swirling, circular patterns that, if you look closely, are actually fossilized snail shells.

This stone has a very interesting origin. Fifty million years ago, sediment formed from runoff of the Rocky Mountains settled in bodies of water. These particular freshwater snails were so abundant that when they died and were washed down into these lakes, entire layers of sediment became comprised almost entirely of their shells. This sediment eventually became fossilized, resulting in this lovely form of chalcedony.

This stone's name comes from an error made when it was discovered. The snail fossils were incorrectly identified as being in the genus *Turritella*. Even though the error was later discovered, the name stuck. The fossils are actually *Elimia tenera*.

Turritella Agate fosters communication with the world of plants and minerals; it aids transitions, insight, and positive thinking. These qualities make this stone perfect for seeing the big picture and releasing worry.

For this spell the stone can be uncut or set into a piece of jewelry. Begin by contemplating what this stone actually is—a fifty-million-year-old rock that contains the shells of living creatures. Amazing. This contemplation can help you gain perspective. Are you overwhelmed by problems and worries? Consider the great expanse of time and how very small we are, how short our lives. Don't spend another minute worrying. Hold the stone in your receptive hand as you chant, then either carry it with you or wear it.

Upon me worry has no hold; I am here, let time unfold.
Never waste a single minute; don't forget that I am in it
for as long as time allows—I repeat these earnest vows.
Wasted time can't be recovered; I am willing to discover
all I know that waits for me—for good of all so shall it be.

Montana Agate Journey Meditation

Montana Agate is transparent to translucent with inclusions that create the look of a landscape. Sometimes called Montana "Moss" Agate due to the shape of the inclusions—they often resemble dendritic or mosslike shapes. The color ranges from creamy-yellow to brown and black with shades of red and orange. This stone is found mainly in the Yellowstone River area.

Like many other agates it fosters a connection to the earth, and it facilitates grounding while stimulating the crown chakra. Montana Agate is especially lovely when held up to a light source. Gaze into your stone and imagine yourself exploring the landscape—this represents a journey. If you don't have Montana Agate, this meditation can also be used with Picture Jasper.

What do you see in the stone? A mountain, or range of mountains? A flat prairie or trees—perhaps both? Or maybe you see layers that represent different planes of existence or worlds. You can imagine that our physical world is the center, the lower world is your subconscious mind or your personal soul, and the upper world is the spiritual plane.

Turn the stone and examine it from various angles—this will change your perspective. When you settle on the view you prefer, visualize yourself entering the stone. If it helps, listen to music or nature sounds during your journey—drumming and singing crystal bowls can also be helpful.

Once you're inside the journey world, let yourself explore. Walk the land and pay attention to what you see. Engage your other senses as well. Spend as much time here as you wish, then record your experiences in a journal. Visit often. Make this a regular place for spiritual journeys. Perhaps you seek a spirit guide or totem animal—see if you can find them here.

Crazy Lace Affirmation for Harmony

Many of the brightly colored agates on the market have been artificially dyed, but not Crazy Lace. It's one of the few agates that occur with naturally vivid colors—usually shades of pink, red, white, and gray. The patterns often contain dramatic wavy lines and circles, earning the name "crazy lace." This is one of the loveliest agates.

Crazy Lace Agate promotes happiness, stability, harmony, and balance. Find a piece you can carry with you (or wear) to keep a positive attitude. When you look at the stone, smile. Imagine those swirling colors surrounding you, lifting your mood.

CHANT:
Buoyant, bright, and light of heart,
every day a brand new start.
Looking deeply I have found
harmony is all around.

Jasper Spells

Picture Jasper Spell to Uncover Fears

Picture Jasper occurs in shades of brown, often with ivory, and sometimes black or blue. Similar to Montana Agate, the patterns on the stone often give the impression of a landscape scene. This stone promotes harmony, stimulates creativity, and can help bring suppressed thoughts or fears to the surface. Due to its appearance, it has been called a stone of "global awareness"—images that resemble landscapes can inspire a collective effort to be mindful of the environment. You can also use the Montana Agate Journey Meditation with this stone.

Place the stone in a small container and cover it with sand. Now think: "What's at the root of my worry or fear? If only I could find that issue and address it."

Speak these words:
Root of worry, source of fear,

Tilt the container and dump off some of the sand. Then say:
I will see you, I will clear

Remove a little more sand and say:
away what hides you; I will reveal.

Uncover the stone completely, then say:
When I find you, I will heal.

Red Jasper Talisman for Progress

Red Jasper is the most common type of jasper; it's good for meditation and dream recall, and also aids progress toward goals, helps prevents setbacks, and promotes courage. It can help one find insight into situations of unfair treatment as well. For this spell, you will create a bundle to carry with you—a talisman to clear the path to your goal.

Wrap the stone in white or red fabric or use a drawstring bag. To encourage success, add nine clover leaves and/or a pinch of ginger root along with the stone. Visualize your goal as you assemble the talisman.

Leopard Jasper Endurance Spell

This stone is also sometimes called Leopard Skin Jasper. It contains markings that appear similar to the coat of a leopard—shades of brown, black, and even red, usually with many spots. Like all forms of jasper, this is a nurturing stone—a stone of harmony. It can also improve one's endurance.

It can be used to bring a sense of calm while improving imagination and creativity.

I like to use jasper when working on creative projects—especially anything that requires stamina. If you have a long-term project you need to tackle, this is the stone for you. This can be anything from remodeling a room (or an entire house) to landscaping, art, or even self-improvement. When you know you're in it for the long haul, let Leopard Jasper be your cheerleader. Wear the stone or carry it. Here's a chant you can use:

The road is long but the load is light;
I endure—goal in sight.
The road is long but worth the walk;
I endure—beat the clock.
The road is long but I take the lead;
I endure—I will succeed.

Other Types of Chalcedony

Carnelian Energy Spell

Carnelian is a reddish-orange variety of chalcedony and is often artificially colored (especially for use in jewelry). The reddish-orange/brown color comes from the presence of hematite (iron) and is translucent but the degree of translucency can vary throughout the stone, giving it lighter and darker patches of color. Banding sometimes occurs as well, which can then be classified as Carnelian Agate.

Carnelian enhances precision and analytical processes and increases one's talents and perceptions. It can help dispel sorrow and apathy, protects against fear and envy, enhances awareness of one's emotions, and stimulates compassion. Carnelian can stabilize the energy of one's home by encouraging love and understanding among family members. It stimulates physical energy, creativity (especially in the performing arts), and passion. You can also use it to clear negative energy from other stones.

The origin of the name is believed to be from the Latin *cornum*—the cornel cherry—because the stone was thought to resemble this fruit. Other sources trace the word to a mispronunciation of "cornelian" from the Latin *carno* or *carnis*, referring to the flesh (like the word carnivorous).

Carnelian is sometimes confused with Sard, a translucent brownish-red shade of chalcedony that has more of a brown hue than Carnelian. Sardonyx is a variety of onyx that has a combination of reddish-brown bands (a blend of sard and onyx). The word *sard* most likely has origins in the Persian word that describes the reddish color—*sered*.

First, place the stone in bright sunlight for at least one hour. Chant three times:

Sun to stone, hold your own,

as you visualize the stone being a receptacle for sunlight.

Then hold the stone in your receptive hand and visualize all the absorbed sunlight flowing from the stone into your body. Feel the energy and power. See yourself glowing. *Chant lucida (Latin for "bright")* as many times as you need—harness the energy of the sun. Repeat as desired.

Bloodstone Talisman for Courage

Bloodstone is also called Heliotrope—it's green or greenish-gray chalcedony with red hematite (iron oxide) spots that resemble blood, hence the name Bloodstone. The name Heliotrope comes from the Greek *helios*, meaning sun, which reveals how this stone, along with many other forms of jasper, has long been associated with the sun and solar deities. It can sometimes be confused with Plasma, which is an opaque form of green chalcedony with lighter (more yellowish than red) spots than Bloodstone.

Due to its appearance, this stone has long been associated with healing blood diseases and curing other ailments. Bloodstone has a long history in folklore, but one of the most popular stories comes from biblical times, when it is said that drops of Jesus's blood fell upon the rocks beneath the cross and turned to stone. It has been reputed to heal wounds and stop bleeding—the stone was actually ground into powder, mixed with egg and honey, and used as a coagulant, to draw out venom and cure tumors. Even gazing upon the stone was said to have healing benefits.

It's referred to as a "stone of courage" and is useful for balancing, grounding, and centering to assist one in overcoming obstacles and personal distress; it's also calming—excellent qualities for a talisman.

You can wear a piece of Bloodstone jewelry or simply carry the stone with you. Charge or dedicate the stone inside a ring of red candles. While the candles are burning, visualize your need and speak your desire out loud or use this chant:

> *Stone of courage, be my shield,*
> *calm and strong, you never yield.*

Chrysoprase: Adaptability Affirmation

Our discussion of chalcedony wouldn't be complete without including Chrysoprase—the most highly prized stone of the chalcedony group. It's translucent to nearly opaque, displays a beautiful apple-green color, and can even have a mint-green hue. It's somewhat rare. Chrysoprase is sometimes confused with Jadeite. *Chryso* is Greek for "golden" and *prase* is from the Greek *prasions* for the leek plant (describing the green color). The presence of nickel is responsible for this lovely shade. Sometimes you will encounter stones simply called Prase. This is translucent chalcedony is a darker shade of green Chrysoprase (which is sometimes used to describe green quartz in general). It can be artificially dyed. Even if the color is natural, however, it can still fade in sunlight, so limit its exposure to any type of bright light.

There's another, rarer form, called Chrome Chalcedony, which is colored by the presence of chromium. This variety is darker than Chrysoprase.

Chrysoprase is an excellent balancing stone. It is especially good for focusing on adaptability and acceptance. It can energize the heart chakra and, in general, provides a compassionate, loving energy.

To become more flexible and accepting of other perspectives and situations, charge a piece of Chrysoprase in full moonlight. Hold the stone in your receptive hand while seeing yourself as more open and tolerant in difficult situations.

CHANT:
In the wind, I gently bend,
I move with ease, like the trees.

– SEVEN –

SIXTH SENSE: STONES FOR ENHANCING INTUITION

Most of us know we have an inner voice that can guide us—our intuition. Sometimes we receive these messages as a "gut" feeling or a sense of knowing something without any logical reason. But what if you're unsure about what your inner voice tells you? Or, what if you can't sense it at all? Because intuition is subtle, we often need help training ourselves to listen. You probably already know that meditation and visualization are techniques you can practice that will help quiet your mind, allowing you to raise awareness so you're open to receiving messages. In addition, intuition can be used to guide spellwork and, of course, divination. Working with crystal magic is one way to help clarify your intuition, and it can also help develop your psychic ability.

You'll notice that several of the stones mentioned here are associated with the element of water and many with the moon or Venus—these correspondences are often used in psychic work and help us become attuned to our feelings. For each stone I have noted subtle differences in the types of energy.

Further associations are provided here based on the stone's internal crystalline structure and, in some cases, referring to the relationship a stone has to the Platonic Solids (see appendix). This gives further uses for each stone and a deeper way to apply the stone's characteristics. Additionally, most of these stones correspond to the third eye (brow) chakra—the seat of insight, self-knowledge, understanding, intuition, perception, and wisdom.

Before we begin, here's a brief primer on the third eye chakra. The chakras are energy centers in the body—the sixth chakra is often called the third eye or brow chakra, an area of consciousness located on the forehead between the eyes. Enhancing this area allows you to see beyond the physical world and access more subtle areas of energy. Learning to focus your attention this way can help you mentally, emotionally, and spiritually—it can also help you see through illusions in your life and gain a deeper understanding of reality.

The actual name of this chakra is ajña, which means to *perceive* and *command*. This chakra can help you navigate your life by gaining insight and understanding intuition, dreams, and symbols. It can help you "see" with more than just your eyes—it can help you "know" and free yourself from patterns that may limit your experience.

Strengthening your third eye helps you see both internally and externally. Your physical vision and your "second sight" are both part of this chakra's energy. See chapter eight for the Dark Moon Journey Meditation, which also assists with seeing deeply within yourself.

There is an actual physical association with the third eye chakra—the pineal gland. In this tiny area of the brain, this gland is a type of "light meter" for the body. Our physical bodies are, in fact, influenced by exposure to light and more than one hundred bodily rhythms are related to this function. This gland also produces serotonin, an important neurotransmitter, and melatonin, which influences sleeping and dreams. You may find it useful to keep a dream journal while working with the third eye chakra.

Enhancing your intuition is an important part of magical practice—it helps you to determine what you should do, along with when, why, and how. Working with all these stones at one time can be overwhelming, so I recommend starting with just one or two. Each stone is suited for particular tasks and settings, so consider your needs and then try a few stones to see which ones work best for you. Combining them is fine, but using more than three or four at a time could result in a lack of focus. If you're already experienced in this area of work, you probably already have your favorite stones. If so, this is a good time to perhaps try something new or experiment with combinations.

There are many ways to use these stones—wear them as jewelry, carry them with you, or simply hold them while you meditate or engage in visualization or divination. You can even sleep with a stone tucked into your pillowcase to encourage dreams. Keep a stone with your tarot cards in a storage box or bag, or place one on top of the deck prior to working with the cards.

I have arranged the stones here based on their internal structure. Three of the crystal structure types are associated with the Platonic Solids (see appendix): trigonal (fire), cubic (earth), and tetragonal (air). These features have a subtle influence on each stone's properties. These categories can help you determine which stones to use. For example, expect possibly more dramatic results with trigonal (fire); stones with a cubic structure (earth) keep you more grounded; those with a tetragonal structure (air) appeal more to intellect and quick movement—these may yield faster results in some cases.

Amethyst

The energy of amethyst is the most peaceful and spiritual of the stones associated with the third eye chakra. It encourages a gentle awakening and is excellent to hold during meditation. Like the other stones described here, it increases psychic ability, although more slowly than some of the others. Associated with the water element and the planets Jupiter and Neptune, amethyst has a trigonal structure, which is associated with fire. This gives amethyst a special "spark" for initiating a journey into intuitive practices. It's a great stone for beginners.

Here's a good meditation to start with:

Dedicate one specific piece of amethyst for working with your third eye. A tumbled piece is best, since it's smooth and comforting to hold. Be sure it's well-cleansed; charge it by the light of a full moon. If this is your first step in working with the third eye, begin by meditating with the stone for at least ten minutes each day. Hold the stone and visualize locating and opening the third eye. Don't try to force any visions, just work on "finding" the third eye and noticing how it feels to be aware of it. Picture the eye opening. Try sleeping with the stone in your pillowcase or hold it against the center of your forehead.

If you're already experienced working with the third eye, you can still use amethyst, but try the Chevron Amethyst to see if you notice any difference.

Chevron Amethyst

Chevron Amethyst, also called Banded Amethyst, contains white and smoky quartz along with the amethyst, banded with stripes that occur in a pointed chevron style. The variety of colors and shapes is incredible, and your collection won't be complete without one. I have several in varying shades of purple; the deepest shades of amethyst are often found in chevron formations, but I do have one that has a great deal of mostly smoky and white quartz. An excellent third eye stone, try it after you've worked with amethyst for awhile.

Just as with amethyst, cleanse and charge a stone that you can dedicate solely for this purpose. The light of the full moon is the best way to charge it. Focus on the opening of the third eye and being ready to accept any visions. If you'd like to chant a mantra, try this:

Open, vision, let me see.
Second sight, come to light.

You can simply hold the stone or lie down and place it on your forehead. Visualize your third eye opening. Remember to keep an open mind. Avoid focusing on any specific questions or problems at this time. Relax and allow the visions to come.

Seer Stone

Seer stones are pieces of quartz that have been tumbled naturally; one side of the stone has been cut away to provide a "window" for gazing. These are most commonly found in clear or milky quartz, but also occurs in amethyst, rose, and smoky quartz. According to Melody, the seer stone can provide access to pre-birth memories and insight into the afterlife.

Charge or dedicate seer stones during the full moon. To work with this stone, practice scrying with it. For a more focused exploration, use this chant:

Let me hear the hidden hints,
let me see the subtle signs.
Help me know the true intent,
help me read between the lines.

Lavender Quartz

As a variety of Rose Quartz, this stone has a very gentle energy yet still heightens instincts. It activates the third eye and promotes clairaudience, clairvoyance, and clairsentience. Like amethyst, since this is a type of quartz, the trigonal structure is associated with the element of fire. This is part of the innate power of quartz crystals—despite the primary elemental association of each stone (if applicable), they all share the subtle influence of fire through their trigonal structure.

This is another excellent stone for beginners; however, this stone has a more varied purpose than some of the others. Lavender Quartz can help with all other forms of psychic awareness. This is a good way to discover your strengths. Are you more attuned to what you hear or what you see? Do you "know" by touching objects? Do you have intuitive dreams? Where does your best intuitive ability come from? In conjunction with this spell, you should also research psychic abilities and find other ways to test yourself.

Meditate with Lavender Quartz, especially when the moon is in Pisces—even better if it's a full moon in Pisces. Here's a chant you can use for focus:

Inner wisdom that resides,
what I need no longer hides—
third eye now will open wide.

Black Sapphire

You may notice that most of the stones included in this section are shades of blue, violet, or purple (or clear). Black Sapphire is an exception. It can help you learn to trust your intuition, calms anxiety, and can relieve self-doubt. It's also protective—wear it in situations where you need to establish boundaries. It can also help you ground and center. Black Sapphire is also good for work with cats and animal spirit guides—especially nocturnal animals. Since it's both grounding and protective, it's a good stone for mediums; it's an excellent shield. Sapphire is associated with the element of water; its trigonal structure gives it balance with power, through its subtle connection with the fire element. It's associated with the Moon and the planet Jupiter.

In general, sapphires are good stones for opening the mind to intuition. After black, blue is the next best choice—it promotes dreaming and astral travel. Sapphires occur in nearly every color—including clear—and are all variations of the mineral corundum, which is from the Sanskrit word *kururvindam* (ruby); in fact, the only other corundum is the ruby (there is a rare pink-orange variety called padparadscha). The only mineral harder than corundum is the diamond. Use this chant with your Black (or Blue) Sapphire:

Grant me wisdom, help me grow—
trust myself and learn to know.

Herkimer Diamond

Herkimer Diamonds are also explored in chapter three, but I wanted to include them here due to their ability to stimulate clairvoyant and clairaudient abilities. A "stone of attunement," Herkimer Diamond helps know yourself, others, and your surroundings, and can help you be present in the moment if you feel stuck in the past or are anxious about the future. Since it's a type of quartz, it has trigonal structure; the fire element can be felt more strongly in this type of quartz formation than other types of clear quartz. Expect quick results from this stone.

Here's a simple chant to use with the Herkimer Diamond. Visualize the outcome you desire.

Know myself, be here now—
let this crystal show me how.

Purple Fluorite

Fluorite increases psychic and spiritual growth along with intuition. It often works faster than amethyst, so it may be more useful for experienced psychic workers. There are no specific planetary or elemental associations for Purple Fluorite. It has a cubic internal structure, which is grounding and practical. Sometimes fluorite appears in octahedron shapes (eight equal sides, like double pyramids)—in this form, they are associated with air. This is a good general foundation stone for psychic practice.

The fluorite octahedron is the best choice for this specific purpose not only for its association with the element of air, but because it's often found in a pure purple color. Many of the carvings of fluorite that can be purchased are a beautiful blend of violet, blue, and green, and, while lovely to look at and excellent for gazing, they do not have the same intense energy of the pure purple. Plus, it's nice to work with this stone in its natural shape. As with amethyst, meditate with the stone each day.

Here's a technique to try:

Hold the stone in your receptive hand or lie down and place the stone on your forehead. Close your eyes and imagine the stone making a connection with your third eye. See it opening, slowly. If you prefer to gaze upon the stone, hold it up to the light and look within it. Visualize your third eye penetrating the stone and searching its depths. Remain open to whatever you see.

Lapis Lazuli

Lapis Lazuli (or Lapis, for short) enhances awareness with wisdom and good judgment. This stone is best for times when you want to stimulate creativity and mental clarity as well as spiritual and psychic awareness. Associated with the water element and the planet Venus, Lapis is actually a rock made up of several minerals, mainly lazurite, calcite, and pyrite, so it can be said to have secondary associations with earth—lazurite and pyrite both have cubic structure.

Lapis is especially effective as a third eye stone (it can also be used for the throat chakra). It's best suited for perfection of the self, helping one find attunement, and developing personal insight. It's the total package when it comes to self-awareness.

Hold or wear the stone and focus on yourself—try to get in touch with your deepest feelings, desires, and even your fears. If something's troubling you, see if you can discover the source—get to the root of the problem. If you're having trouble trusting your instinct, meditate with this stone to seek the answers.

CHANT:
Awakened and aware—
I search myself with care.

Apophyllite

This is the only stone in the list that has a tetragonal structure—associated with the element of air. Apophyllite enhances analysis yet can create a link between the physical and spiritual realms. It can facilitate astral travel and help recall the experience. Apophyllite forms in brilliant crystal pyramids that are excellent for gazing—sometimes the crystals are almost mirrorlike in their reflective quality. It can stimulate intuition and the third eye and can even be used for channeling or to stimulate the heart chakra. Repeat this chant to aid astral travel:

Grounded in place, I'm floating through space.

Azurite

Azurite is often found with malachite, resulting in striking stones that are bright blue with accents of green. Azurite awakens psychic ability and the third eye chakra while helping with decision-making and motivation. Azurite also helps with meditation, creativity, and communication with spirit guides—an excellent stone for vision quests and journey meditations. It also helps one to verbalize psychic experiences, clear barriers, and it promotes compassion and empathy. While it's associated with Venus and the water element, the internal structure of azurite is monoclinic, meaning it offers stability, encouragement, and clarity.

Journey Meditation: Spirit Realm
In a drawstring bag, place a piece of Azurite, a clear quartz point, and another stone that has personal significance for you. If you wish, listen to soothing music, nature sounds, or drumming during your session.

If you already have journey meditations you use regularly, go ahead and use them with this bundle. If not, use this visualization:

Close your eyes. Imagine you are taking a comfortable walk—it can be in the woods, along a well-worn path, or in a field of flowers. Wherever you are, the walking is easy and comfortable. Breathe deeply—note whatever scents are around you—the air is fresh and clean. Keep walking. Notice that eventually the land has inclined slightly. After awhile, you realize you're walking up a smooth hillside. As the hill gets steeper, you see steps cut into the hillside and you climb them. Up and up—you walk easily until you reach the top of the hill. There at the top is a temple and a fountain of water. Linger here and rest awhile if you wish—take note of your surroundings. Drink. Look around—is there anything noteworthy here? Perhaps you will meet a spirit guide.

When you're ready, you'll find another path that leads up a nearby slope, and then, more steps. These are stone, and they lead you up the mountainside. The airs grows thin as you walk, but you're still comfortable. Know that as you ascend, you are getting closer to the realm of spiritual understanding and awakening. Note anything that appears to you along the way up the mountain. When you reach the top, all is white with snow but you're not cold. You can even see clouds drifting by in the perfect blue sky. There is another temple here—take a look around. What do you see? Spend as much time here as you desire. There are many comfortable places to sit. There are other guides here, as well. What do they say to you? What do you say to them?

When you feel ready, walk back down. Again, note what you see and sense along the way. When you reach the place where you started, stop and open your eyes. Write about your experience in a journal. Repeat the meditation any time you wish.

Iolite

Iolite is sometimes called "Water Sapphire," but it's really gemstone quality Corderite. Its gorgeous indigo color makes it much sought after in jewelry. Iolite is one of the major third eye stones (also useful for the crown chakra). It is useful for guided meditations, healing, and astral travel. Iolite can stimulate visions and has been associated with shamanism. The orthorhombic structure of Iolite also gives it the added characteristics of enhancing focus and perspective. Iolite is also used for inspiration and creativity—it aids with self-expression. It can help one escape chaos and become organized and motivated. I have both a tumbled piece of Iolite and an Iolite ring. I have found that charging them together is particularly helpful, especially during a new moon.

Iolite is a wonderful journey stone—it helps one increase the clarity and accuracy of visions, past-life meditations, and helps awaken psychic gifts. This is an excellent stone for mediums, tarot readers, and astrologers. You can use this stone with the previous Journey Meditation but, instead of making a bundle, just carry or wear a piece of Iolite. Try it with the bundle and with Iolite alone and see if you have different experiences.

Kyanite

Kyanite is one of the prettiest blue stones—it can range from pale to deep sky-blue and is noted for its lustrous, bladelike structure. Not surprisingly, its name comes from *kynos*, the Greek word for blue (although it can occur in other colors). It's a wonderful mediation stone—especially if you're one of those people who find it difficult to clear your mind. If you've had trouble meditating in the past, try holding Kyanite in your receptive hand or wearing a Kyanite pendant.

This stone never needs cleansing; it quickly aligns all chakras and is excellent for throat and third eye chakras. It stimulates all areas of psychic ability. I'm particularly fond of my Kyanite pendant that is also set with a tiny clear quartz point. Wearing it never fails to produce a sense of calm and peacefulness.

Kyanite is also balancing, dispels blockages, and helps with dream recall and using dreams to solve problems. It enhances intuition to aid decision-making, promoting clarity and reasoning. It has a triclinic structure that also helps with its balancing qualities.

Make a dream bundle by wrapping a piece of Kyanite in white or blue cloth and placing it inside your pillowcase. Add a few drops of lavender essential oil to the cloth if you wish. Visualize having vivid dreams and remembering them—see yourself being aware in your dreams. In fact, if you've never tried lucid dreaming, see if it will work for you. One of the best techniques is to prompt yourself with subtle clues so that while you're dreaming, you can become aware and realize you're in a dream. Practice these techniques while you're awake—things like asking yourself if you're dreaming or awake, pinching yourself, and looking for a landmark or object. Or simply start keeping a dream journal. Sometimes if you experience a recurring dream, you can program yourself to respond to that situation when the dream occurs again. Chant these words, if it helps:

I will know I'm dreaming,
help me to prepare—
I will know I'm dreaming,
I will be aware.

Kunzite

Kunzite is a variety of the mineral spodumene, discovered in 1902 and named for mineralogist George Frederick Kunz. Kunzite is nearly colorless to shades of pink and lilac (presence of manganese). Hiddenite is the green gemstone variety of spodumene (presence of chromium); spodumene is a noted source of lithium.

For attaining deeper states of meditation, try Kunzite. It also helps you stay centered. Associated with both the heart and third eye chakras, creativity can be stimulated during meditation with Kunzite. It's a very peaceful stone; it can help you remain calm in chaotic situations. It promotes all types of love—self-love, universal love, and romantic love. It also promotes tolerance and straightforwardness. Its monoclinic structure is stabilizing, encouraging, and promotes clarity.

General Intuition Spell

Here's a spell that can be used with any of the stones in this chapter. This is intended for a piece you will wear or carry with you. Charge the stone during a full moon in Pisces, if possible. Visualize and chant:

Listen to the voice inside;
intuition, be my guide.

– EIGHT –

CRYSTAL RITUALS AND SPELLS FOR SABBATS AND ESBATS

As each sabbat rolls around, I look for new ways to decorate my altar and I seek new rituals for the occasion. Incorporating crystals into your sabbat and esbat celebrations can help revive both your crystal magic practice and your seasonal celebrations. While some of these rituals are designed for groups, they can be adapted for individual use.

For a few of these rituals, I have provided Quarter Calls—of course, feel free to use your own or adapt the ones printed here. A few of the rituals also contain evocations and other parts for various speakers. Again, please adapt these as you wish. Most of the rituals are loosely structured, assuming readers will have their own methods of creating sacred space, opening and closing a circle, and blessing cakes and beverages. However, at the end of the chapter, I have provided a Quarter Call and Evocation that can be used for any situation.

Imbolc

Traditionally celebrated with lights and devotions to Brigit (goddess of smithcraft, the hearth, poetry, and healing), Imbolc is also associated with cleansing and purification.

The Old Woman of Winter is transformed into the fair young Bride, symbolizing the lengthening days and growing strength of the sun. February 1 was once called Bride's Day; in Ireland this day was called Imbolc or Oimelc (most likely referring to first milk). Centuries later, this day became known as Brigit's Feast Day and, later, the Christian Church dubbed February 2 as Candlemas, dedicated to the Virgin Mary. Candlelight played a prominent role in all of these celebrations.

There are many variations of Brigit's name, and it's often difficult to separate the Celtic goddess from the Christian Saint Brigit. However, the characteristics are quite similar: she was a great mother figure, associated with inspiration, poetry, healing, wisdom, divination, smithcraft, and other transformative arts. Some lore also includes other skills such as weaving, brewing, and guarding farm animals. She is most often known in her triple goddess aspect—poetry, healing, and smithcraft. Stones for this celebration have been selected based on these qualities.

This is both a ritual to celebrate Imbolc and a spell for whichever qualities you wish to enhance.

Crystal Altar for Imbolc

You will need:

- Three white candles or one large 3-wick white candle for the center of the altar
- Several white tea light candles to create a circle around the centerpiece

- As many additional candles as you like, any size, any color to have in the room (remember, this is a festival of light!)

Any stone or combination of stones from the following list:

- **Agate (Blue Lace)**—inner peace and healing; spiritual awareness
- **Apache Tear**—comfort, removal of barriers; grief acceptance
- **Apatite**—insight, creativity, humanitarian pursuits
- **Geode**—Mother Earth; nurturing
- **Gypsum**—strengthens progress; fertility
- **Jasper**—nurturing and healing
- **Kyanite**—creativity
- **Lepidolite**—stone of transition
- **Malachite**—transformation
- **Obsidian**—goddess mysteries
- **Sulfur**—melts blockages; inspiration

Construct a circle of stones and candles on your altar or tabletop. Depending on how many stones and candles you have, you can alternate stones and candles or place two candles side by side, then a stone, then two more candles. Again, it depends on how many you have and how large a circle you want to create. If you wish, you can incorporate your quarter candles into this circle. Place the three candles in the center (or the large 3-wick candle). When your altar is set, proceed with your usual circle casting or other creation of sacred space. Light the quarter candles, if using, and light the circle candles.

CHANT:

The healing hearth, the fire and spark, the inspiration in my heart—by Brigit's light, the flames ignite, fulfilling what I need tonight.

Light the center candle(s). Visualize your need and focus on the stone(s) representing that goal. When you're ready, close your circle, but allow the center candle(s) to keep burning (you may extinguish the quarter candles).

If you used small candles for the center, allow them (and the circle candles) to burn out. If you used large center candles, allow the circle tea light candles to burn out, then snuff out the center candle(s).

Remove the stones and proceed by wearing or carrying them as desired. These stones can be used in spells for any of Brigit's qualities. For example, I have a Kyanite pendant I like to use in this ritual; later I wear it to promote creativity.

Imbolc Ritual for a Group

Arrange altar and create sacred space as desired. Use stones from the Imbolc list or clear quartz points. Provide a candle for each participant.

Speaker 1:
This time during the yearly cycle is a time for transformation, moving from inner contemplation to outward manifestation, and it was considered by the Celts to be the beginning of the spring quarter: February, March, and April. Though we can't see it or feel it yet, we know life stirs despite the cold.

Speaker 2:
Tonight we ponder a task we face, a project, a desire,

something we have been contemplating on which action needs to be taken; starting a project or continuing and completing something, a seed of desire we wish to cultivate, or any other new beginning we wish to initiate—personal or professional, or both. We join together as brothers/sisters to support each other's efforts. This is a time of nurturing.

When we nurture something, we cherish it, offer encouragement, help it develop, and provide support—whether it's a personal goal, a physical need, or helping those we love.

All:
Seeds are waiting for their day, let our candles light the way.
Day is winning over night, look toward increasing light.
On this Imbolc day/eve we ask, nurture our respective tasks.

Each person lights a candle and speaks about (or silently contemplates) his/her endeavor, task, project, etc., then places the candle in the center of the altar. When everyone has added his/her candle to the altar, each person picks up a stone or crystal.

Speaker 3:
Brigit, we ask for your blessings. Forge for us a strong foundation. May the sparks we ignite here grow into a fire of energy within us. Strengthen our minds, bodies, and spirits— let us approach our goals with your inspiration and passion.

Visualize individual goals as everyone chants together:
Hand and hearth, head and heart, help us make a fruitful start.
All that we endeavor here, manifest throughout the year.

Each person places a stone on the altar, near his/her candle. If using clear quartz points, arrange them so the points face outward.

Enjoy refreshments as desired; close the circle.

After the participants' candles have burned out, each person takes the stone and carries it or keeps it close until his/her goal has been achieved.

Ostara: Spring Equinox

The vernal equinox celebration we call Ostara gets its name from Eostre (or Oestre, Eastre) a Germanic goddess of fertility and sunrise. Anglo-Saxon Christians adopted her name, from which the origin is believed to be the Proto-Germanic word *austron* ("dawn"), from the root *aus*, meaning "to shine." Our word *east* also derives from this, as well as words like *aurora*. It's not too hard to see where the word *Easter* originates. Not surprisingly, it is believed that she was associated with the hare, although other sources indicate she may have had a companion fox. Most everyone knows the theme for this celebration is rebirth and renewal. Popular symbols include eggs, flowers, and cauldrons.

Here's a crystal spell you can perform on the equinox to recharge yourself and boost your energy, revive your spirit, or inspire whatever kind of rebirth you need.

Choose stones from this list:
- **Amber**—increases positive energy
- **Barite**—encourages pursuit of dreams
- **Bloodstone**—improves talents; promotes courage
- **Bornite**—stone of happiness; renews and stimulates the spirit
- **Calcite**—amplifies energy; green calcite for the creative forces of nature

- **Carnelian**—motivation, focus, stimulation
- **Citrine**—optimism
- **Garnet**—self-confidence
- **Gypsum**—fertility
- **Howlite**—take action toward goals
- **Lodestone**—motivation
- **Moonstone**—new beginnings
- **Opal**—affirms purpose; heals spirit
- **Rose Quartz**—love, fertility, and compassion
- **Topaz**—conquer fears
- **Turquoise**—find true purpose

In addition, the following stones are associated with the season of spring: amethyst, emerald, peridot, and pink topaz or pink beryl (Morganite). Of course, you can use any stone not listed here; choose one that suits your purpose.

Crystal Altar for Ostara

After you have selected your stone(s), prepare your altar or other magical space. Use seasonal decorations and symbols—I like to use stone eggs, rabbit statues, and flowers. You can use real eggs, baskets, or anything else that represents spring. I like to put stone eggs on beds of moss to create a nest; you can also use real eggs and create a similar decoration. One year I used half an eggshell I found that had fallen from a bird's nest in my yard—that was truly special!

If you have a small cauldron, place your stone(s) inside. If you don't have one, just use a small dish. Create a display around your cauldron of stones—perhaps arrange several clear quartz points around the base of the cauldron to represent fire. Add other seasonal decorations, candles, etc., creating a celebration of spring. You can add images that represent the type of rebirth you're seeking.

Or, you can put a candle in a cauldron (or use a candle holder) in the center, surround it with moss, and place crystals in the moss—you can partially bury them so they appear to be growing from it. Visualize your goal and chant:

> *Revive, restore, renew.*
> *Let all that I pursue*
> *arrive with spring's debut.*

Ostara/Storm Moon Healing Ritual for a Group

This ritual can be used either to celebrate the spring equinox or the full moon of spring that is often called the Storm Moon.

Altar arrangement:

On a tabletop, create a circle of thirteen small candles—tea lights, votives, or mini-votives—in shades of white, orange, and yellow. If you have enough stones, place one between each of the candles. You can also make this circle smaller or larger, as desired. If you don't have thirteen candles, use six or seven.

In the center of the circle, on a plate or other heat-proof surface, arrange a centerpiece as follows: In the center, use a candle holder with one white candle—votive or tea light. I have a small cauldron I like to use. On either side of the candle holder, if possible, place two stone eggs. To keep them from rolling around, rest them on decorative moss (be sure to keep the candle flame safe from the moss!). Next, add six clear quartz points (facing outward), three on each side of the candle holder. Feel free to incorporate any other stones from the Ostara list. To send healing energy, place two tangerine quartz points on opposite sides of the centerpiece, between the sets of clear quartz points (facing outward).

Create sacred space as desired.

Quarter Calls:
Storm Moon night/Ostara night, spring is near—
power of earth, join us here.
Nurture us, help us grow,
favor all the seeds we sow.
Hail and welcome!

Storm Moon night/Ostara night, spring is near—
power of Air, join us here.
Breath of wind, lift us high,
encourage us to reach the sky.
Hail and welcome!

Storm Moon night/Ostara night, spring is near—
power of fire, join us here.
Spark of life, strength of heart,
empower us for a new start.
Hail and welcome!

Storm Moon night/Ostara night, spring is near—
power of water, join us here.
Wash us clean, fresh as dew,
with the spring, we renew.
Hail and welcome!

Speaker 1:
We are here to celebrate the coming spring (and/or the full
moon), and to raise healing energy for those in need.

Although the land still seems brown and bare, we can see tiny green shoots pushing up, stretching for the sun. The long, cold winter must inevitably end, allowing earth to awaken. Like the land being renewed, we seek to renew ourselves in many ways—especially our health and wellness.

Speaker 2:
Gradually, the days have been growing longer.

Light the ring of candles.

Today/tonight we reach a balance of day and night, and light will continue to strengthen.

Light the candle in the centerpiece.

This candle represents the spring/full moon, and the healing energy we seek for ourselves and our loved ones.

All chant:
Earth is greening, sunlight gleaming;
buds are forming; sky is storming.
Winter's hold, release your hand,
renew ourselves, renew the land.
Restore, revive; mend and heal—
warmth of spring we soon shall feel.

Participants may wish to share other thoughts or requests at this time. Enjoy refreshments, as desired; close the circle.

Beltane

While we welcomed the return of light at Imbolc, now we celebrate life, the growth of the season—sexuality, love, and fertility. A Celtic god called Belenos was associated with the sun and connected with this festival—his name means "bright" or "brilliant." *Bel-tane* means "Bel-fire." The spell and ritual presented here concern both aspects of the celebration—abundance and the power of fire to spark passion.

Use stones associated with the sun and/or the element of fire. Here are some good choices:

- *Fire:* amber, bloodstone, brass, carnelian, citrine, diamond, garnet, gold, hematite, iron, obsidian, onyx, pyrite, rhodocrosite, rhodonite, ruby, sulfur, tiger eye, topaz, and zircon

- *Sun:* amber, brass, carnelian, citrine, diamond, gold, sulfur, and topaz

These stones are associated with abundance and prosperity: aventurine, citrine, diamond, emerald, green calcite (creative forces of nature), malachite, sapphire, tiger eye, and topaz. Use gypsum for fertility.

Abundance Spell

Select your desired stones and place them in a bowl at the center of your altar or on a table. Also add a few stones that you can "plant" in a garden or container to promote growth. Decorate with symbols of the season— lots of green plants, leaves, and flowers. Visualize your specific need or goal, or just focus on general prosperity and vitality.

CHANT:
Lush and glowing, bring good health;
grow and prosper, bring great wealth.
Abundance and longevity—
for good of all, so mote it be.

Bury some of the stones in your garden or potted plant containers; keep the bowl of stones where you can see it every day.

Beltane Passion Amulet

There is a Fire Purging Spell in the Midsummer section; here, we'll use fire for its symbolic spark of passion. Passion can mean many things, including intense emotion of any kind, desire, and enthusiasm. Whether you're seeking a spark of passion in a romantic relationship, or more enthusiasm in your life or work, this ritual can be used for any aspect of your life where you want more passion.

Choose stones that resonate with the fire element and add others that promote passion, depending on your specific goal.

- **Amber**—sensual; increases attractiveness
- **Barite Rose**—aids pursuit of dreams
- **Bornite**—a "stone of hope"
- **Carnelian**—sexual energy
- **Copper**—relieves exhaustion and sexual imbalance
- **Diamond**—imagination and creativity
- **Garnet**—health and vigor
- **Gold**—physical energy
- **Rhodocrosite**—new love
- **Rhyolite**—progress and change

- **Sulfur**—energy and inspiration
- **Topaz**—health, strength, and individuality

You're going to create a talisman to attract your desired outcome. Make a bundle using a drawstring bag or piece of cloth that closes tightly. Add your stones and whatever items you wish to include—herbs, flowers, or a symbol of your intent.

To charge your amulet, hold it while you visualize your goal.

CHANT:
Passion like the fire's flame burn high—
fuel the need I wish to satisfy.

If you don't have access to a large fire, you can simply use a candle or group of candles—use red, white, or both colors. Depending on your situation, large fire or candles, you will either carry your bundle around the fire three times in a clockwise direction, or place your bundle beside the candle(s) until it burns out.

Midsummer: Summer Solstice

This is the longest day of the year and, like Beltane, is associated with fertility, fire, and the sun. Use the special magic of midsummer to enhance your magical potency. These stones are particularly useful for this time of year:

- **Agate**—earth connection and spirituality
- **Amethyst**—increases psychic ability
- **Aquamarine**—enhances psychic ability, creativity, and spiritual awareness
- **Azurite**—connect with spirit guides

- **Celestite**—fosters dream recall and astral travel; spiritual wisdom
- **Chiastolite**—assists with astral travel
- **Iolite**—stimulates shamanic visions
- **Jade**—inspiration and wisdom; gardening
- **Kyanite**—stimulates psychic awareness
- **Labradorite**—balances the aura; wisdom
- **Lapis Lazuli**—wisdom and awareness
- **Moonstone**—intuition and psychic sensitivity
- **Opal**—aids psychic journeys
- **Pearl**—spiritual guidance
- **Purple Fluorite**—intuition
- **Turquoise**—vision quests
- **Wulfenite**—facilitates magical practice
- **Zircon**—spirituality

As with Beltane, here are stones associated with the sun and the element of fire:

- *Fire:* amber, bloodstone, brass, carnelian, citrine, diamond, fire opal, garnet, gold, hematite, iron, obsidian, onyx, pyrite, rhodocrosite, rhodonite, ruby, sulfur, tiger eye, topaz, and zircon
- *Sun:* amber, brass, carnelian, citrine, diamond, gold, sulfur, and topaz

Crystal Spell for Midsummer

You may choose to enhance your magical potency, spiritual connections, psychic ability, wisdom, journeying, astral travel, or divination skills at this time. Charge a special stone or collection of stones tonight—or a piece of magical jewelry. Visualize, focus your intent, and chant:

Light of day is at its height, magic of midsummer night,
charge this stone, at this hour, to enhance my magic power.

Fire Purging Ritual

This ritual can also be performed at Beltane. It can be used individually or with a group. Our coven used this ritual several years ago—be prepared for change!

Prepare sacred space outdoors with access to a fire. I recommend gathering around a fire pit on someone's patio, if possible. Of course, you can do this ritual while camping or even indoors on a smaller scale using a cauldron, fireplace, or wood-burning stove.

Your location will determine how you incorporate your selected stones into this ritual. You can place them around the fire or each person can charge his/her individual stone during the ritual. Individuals can wear a piece of jewelry set with one of the suggested stones or something made of gold or brass. Iron can be incorporated using a cauldron, if you have one. As part of the ritual, everyone could wear a stone bracelet such as hematite. Making simple stretch bracelets is easy; this could be part of the ritual.

Speaker 1:
On this night, we seek the assistance of fire for personal
change. As some seeds require the spark of fire to germinate, so
we ask fire tonight to help us gently clear the way for the new
possibilities we request.

Speaker 2:
We honor the many gods and goddesses of fire: Pele, she who
shapes the land; Hestia and Vesta, keepers of the hearth; Brigit,

goddess of smithcraft and the spark of inspiration; Hephaestus and Vulcan, gods of the forge. We respect the power of fire, and all the elements, and give thanks for this sacred flame.

Speaker 3:
Element of fire, agent of transformation, take now what we purge and help us grow to conquer our fears, overcome obstacles, and heal—in accordance with our highest good, and for the good of all.

Each person writes on paper what she'd like to purge, then throws the paper into the fire.

ALL CHANT:
Transforming fire,
bane to desire.

Speaker 3:
Elementals and deities, we honor you. Accept this offering (herbs and resins of your choice thrown into the fire) to seal our spell.

ALL CHANT:
Hear us well,
seal our spell.

Enjoy refreshments as desired; close the circle.

Lughnasadh: First Harvest

The Celtic god Lugh (or Lug) was known as the many-skilled. He was depicted as being young, attractive, and adept with a spear, sling, and other weapons. He was also a carpenter, smith, poet, sorcerer, historian, and a hero; he was not just proficient in one thing, but many. Lugh represented advancement and newness. For this sabbat, celebrate your many skills and accomplishments and use this spell to enhance your talents. In addition, as it is the first of the three harvest festivals, bread is often blessed and shared at this time.

These stones have properties that include enhancing one's skills, mental or physical, as well as helping one with other practical aspects of life.

- **Apatite**—aids humanitarian pursuits and service to others
- **Aragonite**—fosters reliability and practicality; helps one accept responsibilities
- **Calcite**—excellent for studying; amplifies memory
- **Carnelian**—stimulates analytical capabilities, precision, and concentration
- **Citrine**—enhances mental clarity
- **Copper**—promotes self-esteem
- **Fuchsite**—helps one gain insight into practical matters; helps one adapt
- **Grossular Garnet**—enhances service to others
- **Gold**—purifies and energizes physical body
- **Hematite**—a "stone of the mind"; aids manual dexterity
- **Hemimorphite**—helps one reach potential

- **Herkimer Diamond**—helps with recognition of purpose and identity
- **Howlite**—improves one's character; aids communication
- **Iron**—strength
- **Labradorite**—perseverance and discernment
- **Lodestone**—motivation
- **Marcasite**—stimulates the intellect
- **Pyrite**—enhances memory and understanding; positive energy
- **Quartz with rutile**—stimulates brain function; facilitates inspiration
- **Vanadinite**—facilitates mental processes
- **Yellow Fluorite**—enhances creativity and intellectual pursuits
- **Zebra Rock**—stamina and endurance

Skill Enhancement Spell

This is the perfect time to charge a stone for your special skills and talents. Visualize, focus your intent, and chant:

> *With the skills that I possess,*
> *if I am put to the test—*
> *let me be my very best.*

Lughnasadh Group Ritual

Create sacred space as desired. On the altar, there should be two bowls—one filled with "new" stones (see below) and an empty bowl for stones that represent what is being purged.

Plan for this ritual by having stones that can be given away to participants—clear quartz points are an excellent choice, or any from the list. The "new" stones can also be planned ahead—each person can bring one that represents what they are harvesting and they take their own stone from the bowl. Additionally, have participants bring stones they are willing to give away. This ritual can serve as a kind of crystal exchange. The ritual leader can provide "new" stones to be given away or, if you do this annually, last year's "purged" stones can be cleansed and given away this year.

Each person should bring:

- a stone that represents something to be purged (to give up)
- a stone that symbolizes a current goal or project (to keep)

Speaker 1:
*This time of year is opposite Imbolc—at that time, we focused
on nurturing. This, now, is the time of first harvest and also
a time to begin preparing the fields for the next season. All
things are cycles and in continuous motion, everything touches
everything else—nothing exists in isolation. We know this,
and live each day allowing the wisdom of earth to guide us.*

*As we clear the land, we let go of regrets.
As we nurture and prepare for the next harvest, we ensure
future growth.
As we harvest the fruits of our labor, we celebrate life.*

Speaker 2:
*Those who work the land know that eventually fields need to
be cleared. Sometimes a particular area is not flourishing and
needs to be cleared so it can rest until next year's planting.*

Other fields are abundant and ready to be harvested. And some fields are still growing, not yet reaching their highest potential. Identify these areas of your life. Tonight we begin our harvest.

Speaker 3:
Our abilities and skills aid us in tending our fields. We each possess special talents that we use in our lives. Tonight we honor Lugh, the many-skilled, and give thanks for our many skills and talents. Our abilities aid us in our lives each day and we are grateful for our gifts and do our best to hone them. And as harvest season draws near, we recognize that it takes the skilled hands of many people to bring us this bounty of food.

Go around the circle, each person taking a turn:
- *"This is what I purge."* Put a stone in the offering bowl.
- *"This is what I harvest now."* Take a "new" stone.
- *"This is what I continue to cultivate."* Keep the stone brought with you—place this stone in front of you or hold it.

Each person now has two stones—one they brought and a new one.

ALL CHANT:
Harvest time is drawing near,
may I reap from work this year.
May fruit be heavy on the vine—
abundance flow to me like wine.

Enjoy refreshments as desired; close the circle.

Autumn Equinox: Harvest

This is the classic harvest time—decorations of leaves, fruit, and gourds can be seen everywhere; leaves are beginning to change into their fall splendor. Celebrate the harvest now; give thanks. This ritual uses stones associated with the earth element, as we thank Mother Earth for her bounty and honor those who work the land to help provide us with food.

Stones associated with the earth element include agate, amazonite, amber, bronzite, emerald, fossils, galena, geodes, granite, jasper, jet, malachite, olivine (peridot), petrified wood, salt, tourmaline (green and black), and turquoise. Additionally, sapphire, topaz, and tourmaline are associated with the season of fall.

Crystal Cornucopia

Create a cornucopia or basket of leaves, gourds, nuts, and seeds, and tuck in a few crystals. These look lovely in urns or bowls, too. Artfully arrange the stones so they peek out among the botanicals. Add pine cones, acorns, even dried flowers. Make this your harvest festival centerpiece. For an individual or group celebration, use this harvest blessing if you wish:

Thanks for harvest, blessed yield,
fruits and grain plucked from the field.

I have gained, I have learned,
I've invested, I have earned.
I have given and received,
in hard times, I still believed.

I give thanks and now I ask
to be equal to the task.
Seasons end and start anew—
keep me strong, follow through.

Samhain: New Year

This time is known as the Celtic New Year, a special time that belongs neither to our world nor the otherworld—a time between, when two worlds join. It is a time of the spirits, a time of year considered outside of time and space. Mythology contains many tales of great battles fought at this time of the year, when beings from the supernatural realm would invade and attack the mortal world.

In Celtic lore, Samhain and Beltane divided the year between cold and warm; a year divided by the various tasks of agrarian and pastoral society. Samhain was both a religious and social feast time. People would make offerings out of respect for the power of nature—a power both beneficial and destructive. At Beltane we celebrated the growing time; now, we celebrate the time of repose.

For Samhain, here are some stones associated with Saturn. Why Saturn? He's a god associated with agriculture—and reaping. Naturally, when we contemplate the cycle of life, we also consider death. Also, this list includes stones that have other properties appropriate for this time of year, which is both somber and celebratory. In some cultures, such as the Mexican Day of the Dead, ancestors are honored. In the U.S. we celebrate Halloween with bonfire parties, trick-or-treating, costumes, and other social events. Yet many people, especially in temperate climates, have difficulty with the darkest part of the year and its dreary landscapes and cooler weather. Perhaps we indulge in fun to fight off the fear, the acknowledgment of our own mortality. That's what I love about this celebration—even though it's considered a dark time, it's also marked with some of the most memorable and enjoyable social gatherings.

Try to enjoy the beauty of the barren landscape. I especially love leafless tress silhouetted against the sky, the few remaining colorful leaves falling from the branches, and watching wildlife. When the leaves fall, we're able to see the lines of the tree branches and take a walk in the woods with fewer bugs to annoy us! There's a long winter ahead of us—it can feel like forever until we see green leaves and flowers. We must find ways to enjoy the dark half of the year. Enjoy time with family and friends; work on a creative project.

These stones correspond to some traditional themes:

- **Apache Tear (Obsidian)**—comforting; aids in grief acceptance
- **Black Tourmaline**—grounding; enhances vitality
- **Granite**—see the "big picture"
- **Hematite**—grounding; promotes psychic awareness
- **Jet**—protection; dispels fearful thoughts
- **Obsidian**—goddess mysteries; absorbs negativity
- **Onyx**—banishes grief; heightens instinct
- **Rhyolite**—"stone of resolution"
- **Serpentine**—enhances meditation
- **Smoky Quartz**—transforms negativity; aids grounding; enables one to let go
- **Staurolite (Fairy Cross)**—helps one connect to other planes of existence
- **Topaz**—helps conquer fears

Samhain Divination Spell

Divination is another activity associated with Samhain. Choose a stone (or stones) from the list and prepare your sacred space as desired. Welcome insight that you need to receive. Chant:

What should I know? The stone will show.
Do not conceal—let stone reveal.

There are several ways to practice divination with your stone(s), depending on the type you've chosen. Scrying is probably the best method, but if your stone doesn't have a particularly reflective surface, it may not work. You can hold the stone and meditate for visions, or sleep with it in your pillowcase to encourage divinatory dreams.

Group Ritual for Samhain

Create sacred space as desired. Decorate the altar with stones from the list and a bowl of pomegranate seeds. There should be a candle for each person to light in honor of an ancestor, if necessary, or one candle can represent all and each person may be invited to say a few words about those who have passed on. You will also need one smoky quartz point (use clear quartz if necessary). Ideally, use a generator point that has been previously charged or dedicated for group work. (These crystals have six almost perfectly even faces that meet at the point; they are used to magnify and direct the flow of energy.)

Speaker 1:
We gather on this night to celebrate Samhain—summer has drawn to a close, most of the leaves have fallen, and only a few flowers still cling to their color. Soon, they will rest for the winter; some will return but some will not—even evergreens don't last forever. Yet the cycle goes on. It is that cycle we acknowledge tonight. But just as Persephone learned to be content with Hades and accept her situation we, too, respect the cycle of birth, death, and rebirth. Life decays and feeds new life. We know death is not evil, but inevitable and, like

*Hades, not to be feared. Respect death; respect life. We are here
now and we celebrate.*

*This time of year, Persephone has departed and Demeter
mourns. We taste the fruit to symbolize Persephone's time
in the underworld.*

All chant:
Take comfort; lose fear, this night, this year.

Eat pomegranate seeds.

Speaker 2:
*And to honor those who have completed this journey and moved
on, we light a candle (or candles). May their new path be filled
with light so they may follow it fearlessly and peacefully.*

Light the ancestor candle or have each person light one and take turns
speaking. Pass around the crystal point for each person to hold as he/she
speaks. When complete, place the crystal in the center of the altar.

Raise energy as needed and/or have someone read the poem:

A VILLANELLE FOR SAMHAIN
*A time of change at summer's end—
the wheel has turned, another year.
We touch the night; the dance begins;
this hallowed eve the veil is thin.
We join our hands together here
to usher in the summer's end,*

And share the magic with our friends.
We own the dark, dispel the fear,
we touch the night, the dance begins.

Embrace the tingling of the skin,
the witching hour's drawing near—
a time of change at summer's end.

We whisper to the sky and when
the silver moonlight does appear—
we touch the night, the dance begins.

The energy we raise within
released with our intent sincere.
A time of change at summer's end
we touch the night, the dance begins.

Enjoy refreshments as desired; close the circle.

Yule: Winter Solstice—The Return of the Sun

In spring the celebration of rebirth is easy to see—flowers are blooming and there are hints of green all around. But this time of year it may be harder to feel the subtle shift toward longer days. It's important to harness that hope. This time of year we don't receive as much nourishing sunlight to convert into vitamin D—some people suffer from low energy or even depression during the winter months. Always seek medical attention if there is a serious health concern.

On the day of the winter solstice, get out into the sun if you can or stand near a window. If it's cloudy, imagine you can see the sun. Visualize capturing the light into the center crystal of this layout. It spreads to all the others—and to you—then out all around you, spreading to others, in your home, community, as far as you can see and beyond.

Stones associated with the sun include amber, brass, carnelian, citrine, diamond, gold, sulfur, and topaz. Additionally, clear quartz is appropriate for any crystal magic use, but it's especially nice to use at winter solstice. Clear quartz, diamond, labradorite, moonstone, pearl, and turquoise are associated with the season of winter.

Ritual to Welcome the Sun

To reinforce the returning light, create a spiral sun shape, starting inside and spiraling outward. Use any combination of the listed stones (or all clear quartz) to construct the shape. With each stone you place in position, visualize the strength of the sun getting stronger.

CHANT:
Waning darkness, sun returns, even winter sunlight burns.
Growing rays, longer days, feel the joy as seasons turn.

Fire and Ice: Winter Solstice Group Ritual

This ritual is suitable for day or night. Decorate your altar with as many clear quartz pieces as you can—points, tumbled stones, clusters—go all out! Aim to create the most sparkling display you can. Use lots of candles to catch the light and reflect it—consider using mirrors as well. Make a dazzling display. Feel free to add any other seasonal touches, but keep the focus on the candlelight and crystals.

Begin with none of the candles burning; they will be lit during the ritual. Prepare sacred space as desired.

Speaker 1:
Tonight/today we gather to celebrate the return of the light. Though it is midwinter, we know the days will gradually grow longer and the nurturing sunlight will awaken the earth.

Speaker 2:
Let us not forget, the sun is a star, and we are children of the stars.

Begin lighting the candles.

Speaker 3:
The firelight honors the starlight—we celebrate the sun.

When all candles are burning, all chant:
Harness the light,
sparkling bright,
light of the world,
sunlight unfurled.
Light up the night,
bless us tonight!

Enjoy refreshments; close the circle.

Other Ritual Ideas

Elemental Stones

If you'd like to use stones to mark the quarters or represent the elements on your altar, see the list of Elemental Associations in chapter two. I like to use the following arrangement:

- *Center:* Spirit quartz or clear quartz
- *Earth:* Emerald
- *Air:* Topaz
- *Fire:* Pyrite
- *Water:* Moonstone

Quarter Call

Here's a Quarter Call that can be done by an individual to call all the elements at once:

> *Earth that nurtures,*
> *air that moves;*
> *fire warms us,*
> *water soothes.*
> *Elements, please hear my/our call—*
> *hail and welcome one and all.*

Evocation

This general evocation can be used to welcome the god and goddess into your circle:

> *Mother of the moonlit forest*
> *father of the sunlit field,*
> *wild flowers, wild creatures,*
> *tender seeds and harvest's yield,*
> *perfect balance, sun and moon,*
> *you are with us day and night—*
> *visit this simple circle,*
> *bless this sacred rite.*

Moon Rituals

Every month it's beneficial to set aside some time for our spiritual and magical practice. The full moons and new moons (or dark moons) are the perfect times—time to reflect, celebrate, or simply take a few moments to be thankful.

The new moon is sometimes called "dark," but I use "new moon" to refer to that time when the moon is beginning to wax—even if you can't see it. The "dark" moon is just as the waning moon has disappeared, until it begins to wax again. This is a very subtle difference, but I believe it's important.

The dark moon ritual is for the moment when the moon is completely dark and has not yet started waxing. Consult an almanac for the proper time, just before the moon is considered new.

Each ritual is suitable for an individual or a group.

New Moon Ritual for Renewal

Think of this time as a reboot—restarting yourself for whatever reason. Perhaps you have a habit you'd like to break, or you've stopped a good habit, such as exercising, and you need to start fresh. New moons are the perfect time to hit your personal reset button.

Here's a list of stones that all relate to personal transformation or positive change:

- **Amazonite**—"stone of hope"
- **Amethyst**—spiritual awakening; breaks addictions
- **Aquamarine**—"stone of courage" and spiritual awareness
- **Aventurine**—increases opportunity and motivation; independence

- **Barite Rose**—encourages one to pursue dreams; aids recovery from addictions
- **Bornite (Peacock Ore)**—freshens and renews; "stone of happiness"
- **Cross Stone (Chiastolite)**—assists with change and transitions; problem solving
- **Gypsum**—ends stagnation; promotes awareness of self and surroundings
- **Herkimer Diamond**—harmony and attunement; cleansing
- **Labradorite**—enhances patience and perseverance; "know the right time"
- **Lepidolite**—"stone of transition" and self-love
- **Mica**—aids self-reflection
- **Moonstone**—helps with changes and new beginnings; introspective
- **Soapstone**—widens one's horizons; aids in releasing old routines
- **Topaz**—helps one conquer fears; promote individuality
- **Turquoise**—promotes self-awareness and helps one find "true purpose"

Create a new moon altar with any of the stones from the list. If you have a large number of stones, arrange them in a circle; otherwise just place them on the altar. Prepare your space in whatever other ways you choose, then visualize your need or speak it aloud. It may help if you actually write your goals on a piece of paper and put that on the altar, or use some other visual representation.

CHANT:

*New moon, new start, I will take heart—
begin anew, and follow through.*

Dark Moon Journey Meditation

The dark moon is a time for introspection and self-reflection. The following stones have been selected for their qualities that can assist you on this meditative journey within. Create a journey bundle to carry with you—actually, you'll be holding it while you meditate. Include any of the stones listed here, and any others of your choice.

- **Apache Tear (Obsidian)**—comfort; removes self-limiting barriers
- **Iolite**—spiritual growth; awakens inner knowledge; stimulates shamanic visions
- **Jet**—dispels fear
- **Mica**—aids self-reflection
- **Milky Quartz**—helps one "know thyself"
- **Rutilated Quartz**—promotes insight and communication with higher self
- **Snowflake Obsidian**—sharpens vision; reveals unnecessary patterns; serenity
- **Smoky Quartz**—removes emotional blocks
- **Turquoise**—aids self-awareness and vision quests
- **Zebra Rock**—helps one look beneath the surface

Use this chant before and after the meditation:

If I'm ready, let me see.
When I'm ready, let me know.
In the deepest part of me,
answers wait to help me grow.

I am safe, there is no fear.
I am learning as I should.
As the journey leads me near,
it is for my highest good.

Take several deep breaths and relax. Visualize you are walking down a staircase—down, down, and down you go. It's dark, but there's just enough light to see in front of you—you only see steps. The further you go, the deeper into yourself you become. When you can go no farther, you see a mirror before you. Your reflection has much to tell you, but only when you're ready. Stay there for awhile and see what you learn. Listen to what your mirror self has to say. When you're ready, walk back up the stairs.

Full Moon Ritual

If you have spellwork to perform at this time, you can still create a special full moon centerpiece for your altar. If you don't have a specific spell in mind, use this ritual to simply honor the full moon.

Use whatever base you like for your stone arrangement—something white and round like a plate is perfect. You can also use a mirror or drape white cloth over a tabletop. Create a circle of stones from the full moon list; feel free to accent your arrangement with lots of clear quartz points. Add whatever seasonal decorations you choose, light white or silver candles, and create your sacred space.

Stones associated with the moon: aquamarine, celestite, labradorite, moonstone, pearl, sapphire, selenite (gypsum), silver

Try to actually get outside in the moonlight if you can—try to at least catch a glimpse of the moon. Spend a few moments in silent meditation. Here's a poem to celebrate:

A Sonnet for the Moon

Tonight the moon is asking me to dance,
her glow descends upon the grass and stone,
she beckons me to walk the path alone,
without a question or a backward glance.
With moonlight as my guide I take a chance,
compelled to walk I enter the unknown,
into a forest green I deeply roam,
I move into a mystic kind of trance.
At last I pause and softly bend to kneel,
beneath the trees I touch the sacred ground.
The knowledge light and shadow soon revealed—
to water, earth, and air and fire bound.
By leaf and stone and moonlight I am healed,
the meaning that I seek is finally found.

Enjoy refreshments; close the circle.

Conclusion: Pay Attention

Crystals, like other magical tools, have the power that we give them. They are a tangible symbol of our intent, our goals, and our wishes. Be mindful of this and don't forget about them. Pay attention.

If you have crystals in the home or outside that you haven't tended in awhile, visit them. Cleanse and renew them. If you have boxes of crystals being stored, examine them regularly and keep track of them. When your collection grows to more than 100 specimens, it can be easy to overlook and even ignore them from time to time. I speak from experience, having my crystals stored in decorative boxes, stacked on a shelf. Even though they're stacked neatly and well-organized, I have to regularly open those boxes and remember to use those crystals that don't receive the same attention as my favorites. Like experimenting with different salts and spices, vary your use of crystals. If your collection is small, set a goal to purchase new pieces on a regular basis.

Paying attention means more than looking at your crystals; it means more than mere observation. Attention also means care, consideration, and courtesy, even affection. Attention also means sustained concentration—being mindful. This is a key element of magical practice. Establishing a connection with your crystals is vital to your success. In my previous book I mentioned taking time to "play" with your crystals—study them, hold them up to the light and take a deeper look, use a magnifying glass, photograph them. Connecting with your crystals helps attune you to their subtle energy. No matter how many crystals you have, your work with them is only as good as your connection and attention. Be aware, and be attentive.

Appendix

Stones and Metals: Metaphysical Correspondences

Some sources list stones as having receptive or projective energy. I believe this depends on the type of magic you're performing. Therefore, those correspondences are not given here. However, this information can be inferred based on the element associated with each. If a planetary or elemental association is not given, it is because there is no particular primary correspondence. This list has been compiled by cross-referencing dozens of sources, supplemented with my own experience working with the stones. For convenience, astrological associations have been added here as well (if available). Again, these have been cross-referenced; the properties of the stone are not always an exact match for the astrological sign, allowing for a variety of interpretations. An explanation of crystal systems follows this list.

Actinolite: excellent for shielding; dispels unwanted conditions. Monoclinic.

Agate: general properties: grounding; protection; strength; promotes general good health and longevity; attunement with the earth; calming; personal development. See chapter six. Taurus, Cancer (Turritella), Gemini (Dendritic; Moss), Virgo (Moss), Scorpio (Montana), Capricorn, Aquarius (Turritella), and Pisces (Blue Lace). Trigonal.

Amazonite: balances emotions; "stone of hope," harmony and universal love; eliminates aggravation; helps perfect personal expression. Triclinic. Virgo, Scorpio, and Aquarius. Earth element. Uranus.

Amber (resin): positive energy; healing; sun; sensual; makes wearer irresistible. Gemini, Leo, and Aquarius. Amorphous. Sun. Fire element and Earth element.

Amethyst: promotes sobriety, helps break addictions; curbs passion; encourages spiritual awakening and peace; aids sleep, transformation, and meditation; calms, balances, and clears aura; increases psychic ability. Aries, Virgo, Sagittarius, Capricorn, Aquarius, and Pisces. Trigonal. Jupiter and Neptune. Water element.

Amethyst, Chevron: amethyst that also contains white (milky) quartz and smoky quartz banded in layers with a chevron pattern. In addition to the properties of amethyst, the chevron amethyst is an excellent third eye stone. It can also be used for journeying, self-evaluation, healing, and to promote universal love. Dispels negativity. All astrological signs.

Amethyst, Green: normally amethyst will turn yellow or brown when heated, but some will turn green. "Green amethyst" is a misnomer—Prasiolite is the appropriate name for rare green quartz (can be confused with heat-treated Iolite). Most green amethyst on the market has been heat-treated. Use green amethyst for added healing energy and connection with nature (see also amethyst).

Ametrine: a blend of amethyst and citrine. Promotes confidence and harmony; good for study—combines the calmness of amethyst with the focus of citrine; aids astral travel; enhances creativity; stimulates crown chakra. Virgo and Libra. Trigonal.

Anyolite (Ruby Zoisite): increases one's awareness of individuality; enhances altered states of consciousness; helps one utilize abilities and talents, including psychic abilities. Aries.

Apache Tear (Obsidian): promotes a forgiving attitude; comfort; aids in grief acceptance; removes self-limiting barriers. Aries. Amorphous. Saturn. Fire element.

Apatite: helps manifest insights, especially past life; enhances other stones; related to service professions and humanitarian pursuits; balances; heals; stimulates clairvoyance and assists with deeper meditative states, insight, clarity, and peace; awakens higher self; enhances creativity. Gemini and Sagittarius. Hexagonal.

Apophyllite: aids astral travel; gazing; reflective; encourages spiritual connections; helps one find truth. Gemini and Libra. Tetragonal.

Aquamarine: "stone of courage" and tolerance; protects fishermen; spiritual awareness; psychic abilities; enhances creativity. Aries, Gemini, Libra, Aquarius, and Pisces. Hexagonal. Moon. Water element.

Aragonite: centering; meditation; helps relieve stress and anger; fosters patience, reliability and practicality; helps one accept responsibilities. Capricorn. Orthorhombic.

Aventurine: increases prosperity, "gambler's talisman"; balances male/female energies; general healing stone (especially for pain);

increases opportunity and motivation; independence—"new horizons," luck; creativity/individuality; stress relief. Aries, Taurus, Cancer, and Sagittarius. Trigonal. Mercury. Air element.

Azurite: awakens psychic ability and third eye; eliminates indecision and worry; enhances self-confidence; dissolves blockages; promotes relaxation and awareness—good for use during meditation; enhances creativity and communication with spirit guides; helps verbalize psychic experiences. Virgo and Sagittarius. Monoclinic. Venus. Water element.

Barite "Rose" (also called "Desert Rose"): encourages one to pursue dreams—"all things are possible," encourages independence in relationships; aids detox/recovery from addictions. Aquarius. Orthorhombic.

Bloodstone (also called Heliotrope): a green variety of chalcedony with red (iron oxide) or spots. Purification; promotes courage, grounding, and a "be here now" attitude; balances body; improves talents; enhances decision making. Aries, Libra, and Pisces. Trigonal. Mars. Fire element.

Bornite (Peacock Ore): freshens and renews; stimulates spirit; relieves stress and grief; a "stone of happiness"; protection from negative energy; removes barriers to goals; healing. Cancer. Orthorhombic.

Brass (a mixture of copper and zinc): healing; prosperity; protection. Sun. Fire element.

Bronzite (magnesium and iron): "stone of courtesy" and focused action; attainment and assistance. Promotes peace; helps relieve stress and heal emotional trauma. Leo. Orthorhombic. Venus. Earth element.

Calcite: wide variety of colors; energy amplifier; aids memory; excellent for studying arts and sciences; healing (see also onyx).

Iceland Spar assists with communication; green calcite promotes healing. Cancer and Capricorn (green). Trigonal.

Carnelian: sexuality; personal power; physical energy; stimulates analytical capabilities and precision, concentration; compassion; present moment awareness; focus, motivation, stimulation. Aries, Taurus, Cancer, Gemini, Leo, Virgo, Libra, and Pisces. Trigonal. Sun. Fire element.

Celestite: revitalizing; excellent healing stone; aids pursuit of delicate arts, mental activities, and problem solving; a "stone of balance"; aids astral travel and dream recall; brings calmness and harmony; eases worry; promotes communication and spiritual wisdom; clears chakras; helps distinguish between need/want. Gemini and Capricorn. Orthorhombic. Venus, Neptune. Water element.

Charoite: promotes unconditional love and courage; encourages generosity; dispels loneliness. Sagittarius and Scorpio. Monoclinic.

Chiastolite ("cross-stone"): assists with change, death and rebirth, transitions, astral travel, problem solving, creativity, practicality, and maintenance of spirituality during illness. Libra.

Chrysocolla (a copper mineral): helps one attune to the earth; eliminates fear; increases understanding and capacity to love; purifies home environment; aids communication; a "feminine" stone. Taurus, Cancer, Gemini, Virgo, and Libra. Amorphous. Venus. Water element.

Chrysoprase: Excellent balancing stone; aligns chakras. Especially good for heart chakra. Facilitates meditation; encourages fidelity, acceptance, and compassion. Trigonal. Taurus, Gemini, and Libra. Earth element.

Citrine (a variety of quartz ranging in color from pale yellow to brown): a stone of optimism and abundance; never needs cleansing—does not hold negative energy but dissipates and transmutes it; often called "the merchant's stone," use for success in education and business; aids mental clarity; teaches prosperity; good for community; dispels fear; opens communication/positive influence. Aries, Taurus, Leo, Virgo, Libra, and Pisces. Trigonal. Sun. Fire element.

Copper: energy conductor; promotes self-esteem; aid for exhaustion and sexual imbalance. Sagittarius. Cubic. Venus. Water element.

Creedite: provides clarity of expression in the spiritual realm; helps to remove obstacles toward goal; aids meditation. Virgo. Monoclinic.

Dalmatian Stone: encourages a sense of playfulness and joy, yet still grounding—good for families, children, and pets; strengthens bonds; can help prevent nightmares; protective and healing—excellent for long-term use.

Diamond: promotes courage, purity, and innocence; inspires creativity and imagination; fosters abundance. Aries, Taurus, Leo, Libra, Capricorn, Aquarius, and Pisces. Cubic. Sun. Fire element.

Dolomite: relieves sorrow; helps one understand that "everything happens for a reason"; removes blockages; encourages charity. Aries. Trigonal.

Emerald: "stone of successful love," also encourages prosperity, legal matters, and success in business; enhances memory. Aries, Taurus, and Cancer. Hexagonal. Venus. Earth element.

Fluorite: general properties: promotes order and reason, concentration, and meditation; "stone of discernment and aptitude"; stabilizing; helps one reach height of mental achievement—"the genius stone." Capricorn, Aquarius, and Pisces. Cubic.

Blue: calming energy; orderly communication.

Clear: use for crown chakra; aligns/cleanses aura.

Green: clears negativity from a room—tidying, "minty fresh."

Purple: opens third eye; increases psychic/spiritual growth and intuition.

Yellow: enhances creativity and intellectual pursuits.

Fossil: promotes quality and excellence in one's environment. Virgo.

Fuchsite (green variety of muscovite/mica group): helps one "bounce back"—balancing—use for meditation for insight on practical matters; assists one in adapting to a situation. Aquarius. Monoclinic. Air.

Galena: grounding and centering; "stone of harmony." Capricorn. Cubic. Earth element.

Garnet: "stone of health"; commitment; self-confidence; sexuality; vigor; patience; protects against thieves; sleep with to remember dreams. Aries, Cancer (grossular), Leo, Virgo, Scorpio, Capricorn, and Pisces. Cubic. Mars. Fire element.

Grossular: strengthens stability in lawsuits and legal matters/challenges; enhances service, fertility.

Geode: symbolizes the Earth Mother and womb; helps one see total picture. Virgo. Water element.

Gold: purifies and energies physical body, solar/male energy. Leo. Cubic. Sun. Fire element.

Granite: primarily quartz and orthoclase feldspar. Enables one to "see the big picture" and aids balance in relationships. Prosperity. Libra.

Gypsum: general properties: a lucky stone; ends stagnation; strengthens progress and fertility. Types include alabaster, satin spar, Selenite, and "rose" (crystallized—also called "Desert Rose"); promotes awareness of self and surroundings. (See chapter four.) Aries, Taurus (Selenite), Gemini, Leo, and Sagittarius (alabaster). Monoclinic.

Hematite: purifies and balances; a "stone of the mind"; promotes self-control; grounding; psychic awareness; transforms negativity; carry to relieve stress; aids manual dexterity; helps one achieve goals. Aries, Virgo, Scorpio, and Aquarius. Trigonal. Saturn. Fire element.

Hemimorphite: helps one "know thyself"; decreases self-centeredness with growth toward self-respect and reaching highest potential; promotes creativity; relieves hostility. Libra. Orthorhombic.

Herkimer Diamond (exceptionally clear quartz crystals, named for locality where first discovered, Herkimer County, NY): harmony and attunement; helps one to "be" and know you already are what you seek to become; aids relaxation and expansion of life energy; stimulates clairvoyant abilities; helps retain information/remember dreams; healing; cleansing. Sagittarius. Trigonal.

Howlite: calms communication; helps one take action toward goals; encourages subtlety and tact; improves character; eliminates pain, stress, and rage. Gemini. Monoclinic.

Iolite (blue shades/gem quality cordierite): a third eye stone, use for spiritual growth; stimulates shamanic visions; balances, awakens inner knowledge; can aid one in eliminating debts and accepting responsibilities; good for attaining a healthy constitution; brings harmony to self and relationships; strengthens aura. Taurus, Libra, and Sagittarius. Orthorhombic.

Iron: protection, strength, grounding, healing. Aries and Leo. Cubic. Mars. Fire element.

Jade (nephrite and jadeite, metamorphic rocks): a "dream stone"; also called the "gardener's stone"; increases vitality, harmony, inspiration, perspective, and wisdom; longevity; protective; good fortune. Aries, Taurus, Cancer, Gemini, Virgo, Libra, Scorpio, and Pisces. Venus. Water element.

Jasper: general qualities: "supreme nurturer"; healing; beauty; courage; good fortune and financial success; creativity; harmony; "an Earth Stone"; stabilizing and reduces insecurity; good for grounding after ritual. See chapter six. Aries, Cancer, Leo, Virgo, and Capricorn. Trigonal.

Jet (a form of fossilized wood, similar to coal): protection—dispels fearful thoughts and protects one during the pursuit of business and enhances financial stability. Capricorn. Amorphous. Saturn. Earth element.

Kunzite (a variety of Spodumene): activates heart and third eye chakras. Gentle, loving, peaceful energy; can help remove obstacles, dispel negativity, and is an excellent meditation stone—stimulating creativity. It can help one remain calm in chaotic atmospheres and increases one's tolerance. Scorpio, Taurus, and Leo. Monoclinic.

Kyanite: never needs cleansing; promotes "attunement," tranquility, and aligns chakras immediately. Enhances psychic awareness, clarity, and creative expression; dispels anger and frustration. Aries, Taurus, and Libra. Triclinic.

Labradorite: protects and balances aura; aids in understanding one's destiny; enhances patience, perseverance, and inner knowing; reduces anxiety and stress; discernment in direction—"know right time"; wisdom. Leo, Scorpio, Sagittarius, and Aquarius. Triclinic. Moon. Water element.

Lapis Lazuli: (Lapis is actually a rock consisting mostly of the mineral lazurite, commonly containing pyrite and calcite, among other minerals); a "stone of total awareness"; amplifies spiritual and psychic awareness; promotes good judgment in practical world— wisdom; cheerful; stimulates creativity, mental clarity, and speech; sincerity; self-acceptance; boosts immune system. Virgo and Sagittarius. Cubic. Venus. Water element.

Lepidolite: reduces stress; "stone of transition" and self-love; calms environment; soothes emotions; dispels anger; a dream stone— protects against nightmares; gently induces change to "get to heart of the problem." Libra. Monoclinic. Jupiter, Neptune. Water element.

Lodestone (Magnetite): balances and enhances receptivity to male/ female energies; encourages one to "hold fast" to purpose; motivation; guidance. Gemini and Virgo. Cubic. Venus. Water element.

Malachite: transformation; clears path to goal; protection (especially aviation); business prosperity; soothing; calming; antidepressant; amplifies mood. Taurus, Libra, Scorpio, Capricorn, and Aquarius. Monoclinic. Venus. Earth element.

Marcasite: a polymorph of pyrite—same chemicals, different symmetry; marcasite sold in the jewelry industry is actually pyrite. Promotes insight and stimulates the intellect; promotes spiritual development; guards against impatience. Leo. Orthorhombic.

Mica: self-reflection; aids sleep. Aquarius. Monoclinic. Mercury. Air element.

Moonstone: feminine; lunar energy; "the traveler's stone"; helps with cycles/changes; new beginnings; intuition; insight; healing for women; heightens psychic sensitivity; calming; balancing; introspective and reflective; allows one to distinguish between needs and desires. Cancer, Libra, Scorpio, Sagittarius, Aquarius, and Pisces. Monoclinic. Moon. Water element.

Morganite: the pink variety of beryl, named for J.P. Morgan. Promotes patience and equality in relationships. Activates, cleans, stimulates, and balances the heart chakra. Can assist with earth healing. Helps one act from love, cultivate spirituality, and gain wisdom from one's spirit guides and elders. Libra. Hexagonal.

Obsidian: protective (especially from psychic vamps); good for grounding and scrying; absorbs negativity; promotes goddess mysteries; detachment but with wisdom and love. Snowflake Obsidian: sharpens external and internal vision; reveals contrasts of life to realize unnecessary patterns; serenity in isolation and meditation; "stone of purity"; (see also Apache Tear). Taurus, Libra, Scorpio, and Capricorn. Amorphous. Saturn. Fire element.

Onyx: centering; banishes grief; enhances decision-making; relieves stress; balances male/female energy; aids detachment and self-control; heightens instinct. Leo and Aquarius. Trigonal. Mars. Saturn. Fire element.

Opal: releases inhibitions; awakens mystic qualities; beauty; heals spirit; contains all colors, represents all elements; aids visions and psychic journeying; affirms purpose; can be used to grant wishes and aid magical practice; allows one to fade into background when desired ("invisibility"). Cancer, Virgo, Libra, Scorpio, Sagittarius, Aquarius, and Pisces. Amorphous.

Peacock Ore: see Bornite.

Pearl: faith and spiritual guidance; purity; charity; innocence; sincerity. Cancer and Gemini. Amorphous. Moon. Water element.

Peridot (gem-quality variety of olivine—olivine can be used instead): warm; friendly; furthers understanding of change; use for heart and solar plexus chakras, acceptance regarding relationships. Use for healing. A visionary stone. Can help recover lost items. Frees one from envy; regulates cycles. Cancer, Leo, Virgo, Scorpio, and Sagittarius. Orthorhombic. Venus. Earth element.

Petrified Wood: "Change what you can and don't worry about the rest." Promotes strength, grounding, and past-life meditations; support in times of crisis. Aids transformation; prevents work stress. Leo.

Pewter (a mixture of tin and copper, and some other metals): divination, luck, prosperity. Jupiter. Air element.

Picasso Stone: a type of marble. Promotes meditation, mastery of thought, development of creative talents, and artistic endeavors. Brings clarity to insight; transforms intuition into intellect. Properties of marble also apply—meditation, dream recall, serenity, common sense, and protection. Sagittarius.

Platinum: balancing, centering; emotionally cleansing; enhances intuition. Leo. Cubic. Neptune. Water element.

Prehnite: increases energy and protection. Excellent for use in grids; calming. Aids dream remembrance and divination, especially regarding spiritual pursuits. Orthorhombic. Libra.

Pyrite: shields from negative energy; protective; encourages health; enhances memory and understanding; practicality; strengthens will and positive outlook. Leo. Cubic. Mars. Fire element.

Pyrolusite: useful for transformation of emotional and intellectual conditions; helps to change and/or stabilize relationships; can be used to balance the aura and get to the root of problems. Leo. Tetragonal. Fire element.

Quartz (Clear): clear quartz is often called the "Master Crystal"; corresponds to all elements and astrological signs; promotes balance, purity, meditation, amplifies energy and thoughts; promotes clarity; harmony; a "stone of power"; aids communication on all levels; a magnifier, all-around healer and amplifier; aids focus and transmission of energy. All astrological signs. Trigonal. (See also Amethyst, Ametrine, Citrine.)

Aqua Aura Quartz: clear quartz that has been enhanced with gold. Cleanses aura; activates chakras. Clears negativity. Also corresponds to the properties of gold.

Fire Quartz: also called Red Quartz. Color combinations include red to reddish-brown and sometimes yellow, depending on the amount and type of other inclusions. Hematoid (Ferruginous) Quartz is opaque, deep red, and contains hematite. Other variations include limonite or lepidocrocite. Clear quartz with only minor inclusions of red are often referred to as Harlequin quartz. More grounding than classic clear quartz; especially useful for the root chakra; stimulates flow of energy. Trigonal. Fire element.

Lavender Quartz: because this is a variety of rose quartz (that displays a pale lavender color), it also contains the correspondences for rose quartz. In addition, it activates the third eye; promotes clairaudience, clairvoyance, and clairsentience. Promotes understanding; a loving stone. Aids communication; heightens instincts.

Lithium Quartz: the presence of lepidolite (which contains lithium) is said to be responsible for the violet hue; calming; promotes inner peace, relaxation, and love (see also Lepidolite).

Milky Quartz: stimulates hopes; stabilizes dreams; helps one to know self; clarity of mind; love of truth.

Quartz with rutile: insight; "clears the way;" astral travel; helps to get to root of problem; stimulates brain function; facilitates inspiration; communication with higher self; more intense than clear quartz.

Quartz with tourmaline: creates a "solving" atmosphere; protective; polarity of energy; natural balance.

Rose Quartz: promotes self-love, clarity of emotions, teaches forgiveness, love of others, universal love, compassion; beautifies skin; fertility; sex; cools temper. Taurus, Libra, Sagittarius, and Pisces.

Smoky Quartz: transforms negativity; removes emotional blocks and mental barriers; adds clarity to meditation; balances; grounds; "stone of cooperation;" enhances personal pride and joy in life; enables one to let go; increases love of physical body; activates base chakras. Libra, Sagittarius, and Capricorn.

Tangerine Quartz: the presence of hematite during crystal formation creates a rusty, orange hue. Enhances energy, strength, positive action, vitality, and strengthens the sacral chakra. Grounding; healing.

Tibetan Quartz: found in Tibet; also called "Black Quartz" due to the inclusions of carbon in these crystals. Promotes wisdom. Aids with abstinence and fasting. Good for healing, meditation, and centering.

Rhodocrosite: a "stone of love and balance"; aids meditation; earth healing; removes tendency toward denial and avoidance; promotes health; aids acceptance and interpretation; can bring new love into one's life; emotional balance; unites conscious and subconscious. Taurus, Cancer, Leo, and Scorpio. Trigonal. Mars. Fire element.

Rhondonite: a "stone of love," balances yin-yang energy, attunement with the spirituality of the universe; helps one to achieve greatest potential; activates and energizes the heart chakra while grounding; fosters unconditional love; dispels anxiety, promotes coherence during chaotic encounters; provides calm assurance. Taurus. Triclinic. Mars. Fire element.

Rhyolite: a volcanic rock made up of mainly quartz with other minerals, feldspar is commonly included. Color combinations are usually a mixture of white, gray, green, red, and brown; sometimes it resembles granite. A "stone of resolution"; use for change, variety, and progress; meditation. Sagittarius.

Ruby (Red Corundum): a "stone of nobility"; fosters prosperity and financial stability. Aries, Cancer, Virgo, Scorpio, and Sagittarius. Trigonal. Fire element.

Rutile: works to eliminate circumstances of interference. Taurus and Gemini. Tetragonal.

Sapphire (Blue Corundum): brings peace and joy; a "stone of prosperity." Virgo, Libra, Sagittarius, Capricorn, and Pisces.

> *Black Sapphire:* centering, grounding, and protection; soothes anxiety; helps one trust intuition; promotes employment opportunities. Sagittarius.

> *Star Sapphire (contains rutile):* centering; wisdom; good fortune. Libra, Sagittarius, and Capricorn. Trigonal. Moon. Water element.

> *Yellow:* wealth, ambition, and endurance. Leo.

> *Green:* loyalty and dream recall. Gemini and Leo.

Septarian Nodule: aids communication and connection with the earth; stimulates creativity, vitality, and clarity—contains the combined properties of aragonite and calcite. Helps one see the "big picture" and enjoy the journey.

Serpentine (a group of rocks that display a greenish, scalelike appearance, usually containing magnesium and iron): enhances meditative state; clears chakras; assists disorders in body and emotion with conscious direction to problem. Gemini. Saturn. Fire element.

Silver: enhances mental function; soothes anger; aids circulation; relieves stress; emotional balance; improves speech; excellent energy conductor; associated with moon; female energies. Cancer and Aquarius. Cubic. Moon. Water element. Receptive.

Soapstone (Steatite): promotes ambition and motivation; allows one to release old routines and expand one's horizons; calming yet encourages action; prepares one for change. Sagittarius.

Sodalite: logic, clarity; encourages objectivity; aids sleep; eliminates confusion; promotes fellowship; self-esteem; trust; helps one to verbalize true feelings; clears mind; helps to reach logical conclusions; helps you "lighten up." Cancer, Virgo, and Sagittarius. Cubic. Venus. Water element.

Staurolite: known for twinning habit of crystals giving the name "Fairy Cross" to these formations. A good-luck talisman; can facilitate rituals, magic, and connection with other planes of existence. Stress relief. Pisces. Monoclinic.

Sulfur: promotes an abundance of energy, flashes of inspiration, and stimulates the application of devotion toward realization of the perfection of the self; helps to gently "melt" barriers blocking progress. Leo. Orthorhombic. Sun. Fire element.

Tiger Eye (or Tiger's Eye; a variety of quartz): focus and concentration; perception, understanding; grounding; wealth and money talisman; protection; psychic sight and insight; courage and strength; optimism—helps one to see things in the best light; slight masculine energy; balances; enhances creativity, integrity, and personal power; helps one manifest ideas into reality.

> *Blue:* this variety is often referred to as Falcon's Eye or Hawk's Eye; promotes peace and healing.

> *Red:* protection (red is usually heat-treated for color). Gemini, Virgo, Capricorn, and Aquarius (blue). Trigonal. Sun. Fire element.

Tiger Iron: A combination of golden tiger eye, red jasper, and hematite. Additional properties include enhancing creativity and artistic ability; energetic—stimulates vitality. Leo.

Tin: promotes new beginnings; divination; good fortune; prosperity. Taurus, Libra, and Sagittarius. Tetragonal. Jupiter. Air element.

Topaz: helps to conquer fears; a "stone of true love and success in all endeavors"; promotes individuality and creativity; helps one trust decisions and see "big picture"; wealth and health; trust; strength; protection; increases abstract thought. Leo, Scorpio, Sagittarius, and Aquarius (blue). Orthorhombic. Sun. Fire element.

Tourmaline: Black: protects against negative energy—energy deflector; enhances physical vitality; practicality; creativity; grounding; reflects negative spells. Watermelon: super activator of heart chakra; allows for experience of beauty of nature; treats nervousness and emotional disorders; enhances cooperative efforts; balance; helps one to recover from heartache. Gemini (watermelon), Virgo (watermelon), Libra, Sagittarius, Taurus (blue), and Aquarius (blue). Trigonal.

Turquoise: encourages spiritual attunement; use as a guide during vision quests (protection); grounding; wisdom; kindness; promotes clarity in communication; eases anxiety; aids self-awareness; helps one find "true purpose." Gemini, Libra, Scorpio, Sagittarius, Aquarius, and Pisces. Triclinic. Venus, Neptune. Earth element.

Ulexite (also known as TV rock or TV stone): fosters clarity and problem-solving; helps one attune with self and gain insight; stimulates third eye, creativity, and imagination. Triclinic. Gemini.

Unakite: heart chakra and healing; emotional balance; more grounding than rose quartz; awakens love within. Scorpio.

Vanadinite: facilitates mental processes; bridges thought and intelligence; can provide for a deep meditative state; promotes order and thrift in spending. Virgo. Hexagonal.

Wulfenite: facilitates magical practice; allows for one to continue despite potential roadblocks or limitations; provides transition to psychic and astral planes. Sagittarius. Tetragonal.

Zebra Stone or Zebra Rock (quartz and basalt): stamina; endurance (especially for athletes); gives strength in difficult times; dismisses anger; brings compassion and understanding; "look beneath the surface"; activate during full or new moon cycle. Taurus and Gemini.

Zircon (not to be confused with cubic zirconia, which is synthetic): "stone of virtue"; a spiritual stone, innocence and purity; can help align chakras. Tetragonal. Taurus, Leo, Virgo, and Sagittarius (blue).

Zoisite: named for its discoverer—Baron von Zois. Dispels idleness; transforms negative energy. Orthorhombic.

Crystal Systems

There are seven basic crystal systems and these can be further divided into 32 classes based on various combinations of this structure. For our purposes, we'll only consider the basic seven systems. Crystal habit is the term used to describe the crystal's outward appearance. Think of it this way: system or structure is internal, a habit is external—like a habit a person exhibits.

These seven systems of crystal structure are important because, in magic, numerology and shapes carry meaning. For example, the cube is often used as a symbol for earth and a pyramid is used to represent fire. Crystals with this particular type of structure can be used for magic related to these elements.

Remember, these systems describe the internal structure that may or may not be apparent in the actual shape of the crystal. In addition, these specific shapes offer particular characteristics we can incorporate into crystal magic.

Cubic (also called isometric)—Basically, this is a cube; a three-dimensional square. Six square faces at 90-degree angles to each other. This form is also called hexahedron (fancy way of saying six sides). This structure can actually have 15 different forms—more than any of the other crystal systems. This structure has the highest degree of crystalline symmetry. This group includes diamond, halite (rock salt), sodalite, garnet, fluorite, gold, silver, copper, platinum, and pyrite. Lapis Lazuli also has this structure, but this mineral rarely crystallizes (lapis is more accurately classified as a rock). Sometimes these minerals really do form cube shapes—think of pieces of pyrite or fluorite you've seen. The ultimate form of stability and firm foundation, this form, no matter what stone it is, can provide a grounding effect or be used in spells and grids for practical purposes, reality, and structure.

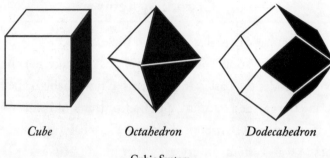

Cube   *Octahedron*   *Dodecahedron*

Cubic System

Note: An octahedron is a shape that falls into this category. I mention this because fluorite octahedron crystals are common among collectors. Here's the confusing part—even though you may have an eight-sided fluorite octahedron, it has a cubic atomic structure inside. The symmetry of the atoms determines what kind of shape the crystal will take, but this arrangement has many possibilities.

Tetragonal—Imagine a cube being stretched at top and bottom. This is a system of three axes that meet at right angles; two are of equal length and the third is either longer or shorter. This system is based on a rectangular structure and includes shapes such as four-sided prisms and pyramids, and eight-sided and double pyramids. Crystals that display this structure are zircon, apophyllite, wulfenite, and rutile. The characteristics of this form can help with balancing or uniting opposing forces.

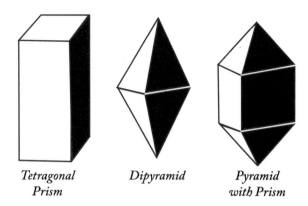

Tetragonal Prism   *Dipyramid*   *Pyramid with Prism*

Tetragonal System

Orthorhombic—The orthorhombic system of crystals is similar to the tetragonal system in that there are three axes that are perpendicular to each other; however, the three axes are all unequal in length. These axes of different lengths meet at right angles and are based on a diamond-shaped inner structure. Shapes include rhombic prism and pyramid. Crystals in this group include barite, sulfur, topaz, celestite, iolite, hemimorphite, aragonite, and peridot. This form helps with focus and perspective in a situation.

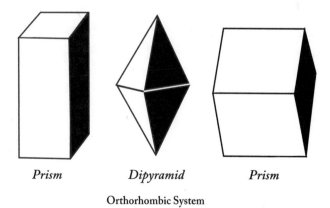

Prism   *Dipyramid*   *Prism*

Orthorhombic System

Monoclinic—This system has three axes of different lengths. Two are at right angles and the third is inclined. This structure is based on the parallelogram. Crystals in this group are azurite, malachite, howlite, moonstone, serpentine, chrysocolla, gypsum, mica (muscovite), lazulite, staurolite, talc, jadite, selenite, lepdiolite, and kunzite. This form is stabilizing, encouraging, and often used to obtain clarity.

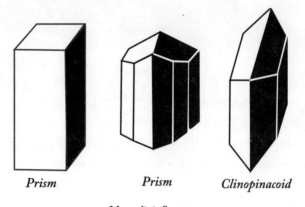

Prism   *Prism*   *Clinopinacoid*

Monoclinic System

Triclinic—This system contains three axes of different lengths that form a pair of faces parallel to the axes and is based on a structure of three inclined angles. Crystals in this group include turquoise, amazonite, labradorite, rhodonite, and kyanite. This is the least symmetric of the group, often producing tabular-style crystals. This form can assist with balance in one's personal life, perceptions, and attitudes.

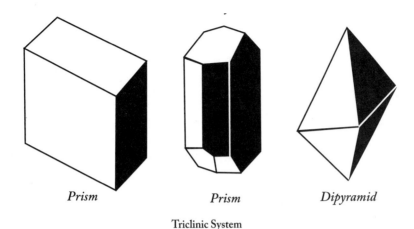

Prism   *Prism*   *Dipyramid*

Triclinic System

Hexagonal—A system of four axes, one of which is shorter than the other three. These three are the same length and meet at right angles of 60 degrees. This arrangement is based on a six-sided internal structure and has seven planes of symmetry, seven axes, and a center. Some common crystal shapes are six-sided points, plus four-sided pyramids and prisms, twelve-sided pyramids, and double pyramids. Many varieties of crystals can be produced by this structure. Examples of hexagonal minerals are: emerald, aquamarine, apatite, and vanadinite. This form aids with vitality, growth, and intuition.

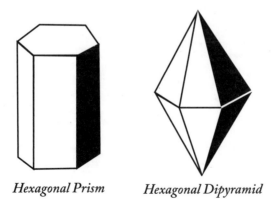

Hexagonal Prism   *Hexagonal Dipyramid*

Hexagonal System

Trigonal—This system is similar to the hexagonal and is often listed as a subset of hexagonal. This system is based on a triangular structure and shapes include three-sided prisms and pyramids and rhombohedra. Crystals in this group include all varieties of quartz, sapphire, agate, calcite, carnelian, dolomite, hematite, ruby, tourmaline, onyx, bloodstone, and rhodochrosite. This form helps stimulate a balancing type of energy and is similar to hexagonal, but with a more powerful force. Trigonal has two lattice systems— hexagonal and rhombohedral.

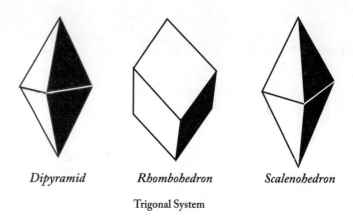

Dipyramid   *Rhombohedron*   *Scalenohedron*

Trigonal System

Speaking of symmetry, only a sphere has perfect symmetry and this form is not naturally found in crystals. If we want one, we have to carve the stone into that shape.

Amorphous materials lack symmetrical atomic structure (some of these are organic substances rather than minerals). They include amber, chrysocolla, jet, obsidian, opal, and pearl.

Platonic Solids

Plato's studies about the universe were not based on an actual study of science, but he proposed the idea that the qualities of things in the physical world reflected pure and perfect ideas. This is how he came to his philosophy of these five "perfect" geometric shapes. He claimed these shapes made up the entire structure of the world—the elements and the universe. Of course, we now understand this is not scientifically true, but Plato's idea of these shapes did, in fact, touch upon crystal structure. In fact, these forms were not actually discovered by Plato—they were actually known thousands of years prior to his "discovery"—stone models of these shapes have been found in the British Isles and appear to be almost 4,000 years old!

These shapes are unique because they have certain characteristics: they have the same shape on each side, every line is the same length, every internal angle is the same, and each fits perfectly within a sphere. They also have duality.

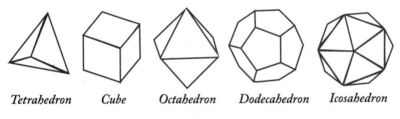

| *Tetrahedron* | *Cube* | *Octahedron* | *Dodecahedron* | *Icosahedron* |

Platonic Solids

They are regular polyhedra (many faces) or many "seats" and they are the five regular, convex, three-dimensional solids. *In crystal structure, only three of the five Platonic Solids occur naturally—the tetrahedron, cube, and octahedron.* (Remember, this is internal structure, not necessarily the outward appearance of the stone. However, some stones do display this outward shape.) When working with the metaphysical properties of stones, it's useful to consider these crystalline forms.

Here are the characteristics attributed to each of the Platonic Solids:

- **Tetrahedron (a pyramid)**—four equal triangular faces—Fire/Plasma (trigonal)

  » all faces are triangular—the base does not have a square bottom.

  » apophyllite (often forms natural pyramids); sometimes zircon.

- **Cube**—six square faces—Earth/Solid (cubic)

  » table salt (sodium chloride/halite) forms natural cubes; pyrite is another good example.

- **Octahedron (dual square-bottomed pyramids)**—eight equal triangular faces—Air/Gas (tetragonal)

  » fluorite is often found in this shape; diamond, too. But remember, these minerals have an internal structure that is cubic—the habit (outward appearance) is sometimes octahedral.

- **Dodecahedron**—twelve pentagonal faces—(Universe/Vacuum) a very mystical shape—twelve pentagons (12 perfect, five-sided shapes)

- **Icosahedron**—twenty equal triangular faces—Water/Liquid

Don't confuse tetrahedron with tetragronal. *Tetra* comes from Greek and means "four" but these are different things: a tetrahedron has four triangular faces; the tetragonal crystal system has two internal lattice systems—one is a stretched cube and the other is a prism. The word *tetra* is used because there are four points on the lattice. Think of a square shape (not cube) that has four points. Repeating points on an invisible lattice create the symmetry.

Planetary Associations

Sun: amber, brass, carnelian, citrine, diamond, gold, sulfur, tiger eye, topaz, zircon

Moon: aquamarine, celestite, gypsum (selenite), labradorite, moonstone, pearl, quartz (clear and milky), sapphire, silver

Mercury: agate, aventurine, citrine, mica, opal and fire opal, serpentine

Venus: azurite, beryl, chrysocolla, chrysoprase, calcite (blue, pink, green), copper, emerald, jade, lapis lazuli, lodestone, malachite, olivine (peridot), sodalite, tourmaline (blue, green, pink, and watermelon), turquoise

Mars: bloodstone, flint, garnet, magnetite, iron, pyrite, red jasper, rhodochrosite, rhodonite, ruby

Jupiter: amethyst, lapis lazuli, lepidolite, pewter, sapphire, tin

Saturn: Apache tear, galena, hematite, jet, obsidian, onyx, salt, serpentine, tourmaline (black)

Uranus: amazonite

Neptune: amethyst, lepidolite, platinum, turquoise

Correspondences for Days
of the Week: Stones, Incense, and Oils

Sunday/Sun/Success, Healing, Protection, Energy

Stones: amber, carnelian, citrine, diamond, gold, sulfur, tiger eye, topaz

Incense/Oils: benzoin, cinnamon, copal, frankincense, rosemary

Monday/Moon/Spirituality, Intuition, Emotions, Dreams, Peace, Meditation

Stones: aquamarine, labradorite, moonstone, pearl, sapphire, selenite (gypsum), silver

Incense/Oils: eucalyptus, jasmine, lemon, myrrh, sandalwood

Tuesday/Mars/Protection, Strength, Courage, Sexual Energy, Healing

Stones: bloodstone, garnet, iron, pyrite, rhodochrosite, rhodonite

Incense/Oils: dragon's blood, pine

Wednesday/Mercury/Communication, Travel, Study

Stones: aventurine, mica

Incense/Oils: lavender, lemongrass, peppermint

Thursday/Jupiter/Prosperity, Expansion

Stones: amethyst, lepidolite

Incense/Oils: star anise

Friday/Venus/Love, Abundance, Nurturing, Beauty, Happiness, Friendship

Stones: azurite, chrysocolla, celestite, copper, emerald, jade, lapis lazuli, lodestone, malachite, peridot, sodalite, turquoise

Incense/Oils: rose, spearmint, spikenard, vanilla

Saturday/Saturn/Longevity, Grounding, Wisdom, Purification

Stones: Apache tear, hematite, jet, serpentine, obsidian, onyx

Incense/Oils: patchouli

Chakra Stones

Root
Color: Red

Stones: agate, bloodstone, garnet, hematite, red jasper, onyx, rhodonite, ruby, tiger eye, tourmaline (black)

Stimulates life force; energy, vitality. Work with this chakra if you need assistance with addiction, diminished sexuality, digestive disorders. This area fosters a connection with nature. Linked to reproductive glands. Grounding. Earth element. Resting place of the life force. Associated with the sense of smell.

Sacral
Color: Orange

Stones: carnelian, citrine, jasper, moonstone, tangerine quartz, tiger eye

Governs the body's liquid elements—work with this chakra if you have problems with sex, nourishment, circulation, or balance. Linked to adrenaline—fight or flight (stress). Creativity, sexuality, authority, and power. Water element. Associated with the sense of taste.

Solar Plexus
Color: Yellow

Stones: tiger eye, topaz, citrine, rose quartz, septarian nodule, aventurine quartz, malachite

Treat discontent, restlessness, and discouragement; fosters inner peace. Fire element. Pancreas, liver, stomach—individuality, personal power, link between mind and emotion. Digestive system and autonomic nervous system. Associated with sense of sight.

Heart

Color: Green (sometimes pink)

Stones: aventurine, chrysoprase, emerald, jade, lithium quartz, morganite, moss agate, olivine, green and watermelon tourmaline, rhodonite, rhodochrosite, rose quartz, unakite

Empathy, joy, friendship, heart, compassion, circulation, thymus gland, immune system. Air element. "Higher" emotions: tenderness, compassion, unconditional love, universal truth. Rules the heart, lungs, upper chest, back, and bronchial tubes. Associated with sense of touch.

Throat

Color: Blue

Stones: aquamarine, azurite, celestite, chrysocolla, lapis lazuli, moonstone, opal, blue topaz, pearl, turquoise

Helps one open to new experiences and self-expression; governs the thyroid, hunger, thirst, eyes, ears, nose, throat, lungs, voice, and speech. Element: Ether. Communication—writing, speech, and art. Associated with the sense of hearing.

Third Eye/Brow

Color: Indigo

Stones: amethyst, azurite, fluorite (purple), iolite, kyanite, lapis lazuli, sapphire (especially blue and black), sodalite, clear quartz (especially Herkimer diamond), ulexite

Understanding and insight, intuition, self-knowledge, perception; eyes, nose, face, senses; mysticism; telepathic energy. Associated with the "sixth sense"—insight and wisdom.

Crown

Color: Violet

Stones: amethyst, ametrine, calcite (golden), celestite, clear quartz, diamond, gold, clear fluorite (or violet), lithium quartz

Inner development, spirituality, enlightenment; seat of the soul—perfection of body, mind, and spirit—cosmic energy. Transmutation.

Seasonal Associations

Spring: amethyst, emerald, pink topaz, peridot

Summer: garnet, fire opal, ruby

Autumn: sapphire, topaz, tourmaline

Winter: diamond, labradorite, moonstone, pearl, clear quartz, turquoise, pearl

Stones by Use

Here is a listing of groups of stones commonly used for a purpose. Keep in mind that each stone has subtle differences—I have noted some of the more important distinctions here. Start here for quick reference by topic, then examine the properties of each stone to fine-tune your choice.

Attraction/Lust

amber, carnelian, jasper (beauty)

Balancing

apatite, aventurine, bloodstone, bornite, celestite, clear quartz, dolomite, hematite, labradorite (aura), lodestone, moonstone, onyx, platinum, pyrolusite (aura), rhodocrosite, silver, smoky quartz, tiger eye, turquoise, tourmalinated quartz, watermelon tourmaline, unakite (emotional)

Cleansing/Purification

aqua aura quartz (aura), citrine, chrysocolla (home), clear quartz, blue fluorite (aura), green fluorite, gold, Herkimer diamond, kyanite

Creativity

ametrine, apatite, aquamarine, aventurine, azurite, celestite, diamond, jade (nephrite), kunzite, kyanite, lapis lazuli, Picasso stone, sodalite, stillbite, tiger eye, blue topaz, turquoise, ulexite, yellow fluorite

Communication

creedite (in spirit realm), howlite, lavender quartz, sodalite

Dispel Negativity, Dissolve Blockages, Increase Positive Energy and Happiness

amber, apatite, aqua aura quartz, calcite, carnelian (energy), clear quartz, celestite, copper (conductor), black tourmaline, bornite ("stone of happiness"), Dalmatian stone, dolomite, green fluorite, gypsum, hematite, kunzite, malachite, obsidian, peridot, pyrite, silver (conductor), smoky quartz, sulfur, tiger eye, topaz, turquoise, zebra stone, zoisite

Grounding, Centering, Focus

agate, carnelian, black tourmaline, bloodstone ("be here now"), fluorite, galena, hematite, iron, jasper, lodestone (direction/guidance), obsidian, smoky quartz, tangerine quartz, Tibetan quartz, tiger eye

Love and Relationships

charoite (generosity; unconditional love) Dalmatian stone (family and bonds), emerald, kunzite, lavender quartz, lithium quartz, morganite (relationships), pyrolusite (relationships), rhodonite, rhodocrosite, rose quartz (universal/gentle love), unakite (grounding and emotionally balancing)

Note: Rhodocrosite (manganese ore) and Rhodonite are often confused with one another. Both can be used for love; both are ruled by Mars and the element of fire, so they're stronger in love spells than rose quartz—more passion-oriented. Both are used for balanced love. Rhodonite is more directed as self-love and unconditional love; Rhodocrosite brings new love into one's life, can help facilitate earth healing, and aids acceptance—an excellent stone for balancing. The "rhodo" in both names refers to the rose color. Rhodocrosite is generally prettier, often streaked with white calcite, and can form crystals. Rhodonite is more grounding and harder, often associated with pyrite or display veins of black manganese; crystals are rare.

Harmony, Hope, and Peace

ametrine, clear quartz, galena, Herkimer diamond, kunzite, lithium quartz (peace), opal, peridot, Picasso stone, stillbite

Meditation

amethyst, azurite, clear quartz, fluorite, kunzite, lithium quartz, petrified wood (past lives), Picasso stone, rhodocrosite, serpentine, smoky quartz, snowflake obsidian, Tibetan quartz, vanadinate

Prosperity/Success

aqua aura quartz, aventurine, brass, citrine, diamond, emerald, gold, malachite, pewter, rhodonite (reach potential), tiger eye

Fertility

grossular garnet, gypsum, rose quartz

Good Fortune

aventurine, gypsum, jasper, pewter, staurolite (fairy cross), topaz

Healing (General)

amber, clear quartz, bloodstone (blood), bronzite (emotional), calcite, celestite, Dalmatian stone, gold, Herkimer diamond, iron, jasper (supreme nurturer), moonstone (women), morganite (Earth healing), peridot, unakite

Health/Longevity, Energy

agate, brass, garnet, jade, lapis lazuli (immune system), pyrite, rhodocrosite, tangerine quartz, tiger eye, topaz

Mental Acuity, Intellect, Wisdom

anyolite (talents), apatite, aquamarine, bloodstone (decisions), calcite, carnelian, celestite, citrine, clear quartz, fluorite, hematite, Herkimer diamond, jade, lapis lazuli, milky quartz, Picasso stone, pyrite (memory), rutilated quartz, silver, sodalite, Tibetan quartz, tiger eye, topaz, tourmalinated quartz, vanadinite, zebra rock

Protection

actinolite, agate, black tourmaline, bloodstone, brass, clear quartz, Dalmatian stone, garnet, iron, jade, lepidolite (nightmares), malachite (air travel), moonstone (travel), obsidian, Picasso stone, pyrite, tiger eye, turquoise

Psychic Ability, Awareness, Insight, Intuition

anyolite, apatite, azurite, apophyllite, calcite, celestite, hematite, Herkimer diamond, kyanite, labradorite, lapis lazuli, lavender quartz, moonstone, opal, pewter (divination), prehnite, purple fluorite, sapphire (black and blue), silver, tiger eye. Third Eye Stimulation: amethyst (and chevron amethyst), apatite, apophyllite, azurite, fluorite (purple), Herkimer diamond, iolite, kyanite, lapis lazuli, lavender quartz, moonstone, opal, quartz (clear), ulexite, wulfenite

Recover Lost Objects
peridot

Sleep/Dreams
amethyst, celestite, garnet, jade, lepidolite (guard against nightmares), mica, milky quartz, sodalite, topaz

Spirituality
amethyst, apophyllite, aquamarine, celestite, chiastolite (during illness), clear quartz, creedite (communication in spirit realm), diamond, morganite, opal, prehnite, Shiva Lingam stone, Tibetan quartz, turquoise (vison quests/journey)

Strength, Courage, Confidence, Self-Esteem
agate, ametrine, aquamarine ("stone of courage"), azurite, barite rose, charoite, citrine, copper (self-esteem), garnet, iron, leopard jasper (courage), picture jasper, sodalite, tangerine quartz, topaz, lapis lazuli, zebra rock (physical endurance)

Stress-Relief/Anxiety-Relief,
Ease Emotional Disorders, Relaxation, Calming
agate (blue lace, turritella), amazonite, amethyst, aventurine, azurite, blue fluorite, bornite, copper, diamond, jasper, Herkimer diamond, kunzite, kyanite, labradorite, lithium quartz, malachite, moonstone, onyx, petrified

wood (work environments), platinum, prehnite, rhodonite, rose quartz, septarian nodule, silver, staurolite (fairy cross), turquoise, unakite, watermelon tourmaline

Transitions/Transformation, Comfort, Self-Reflection

amethyst, Apache tear, chiastolite, lepidolite, lithium quartz, malachite, mica, petrified wood, rhodocrosite, soapstone, sulfur, tin (new beginnings)

Travel

ametrine (astral), apophyllite (astral), chiastolite (astral), moonstone, turquoise (shamanic journeying/vision quests)

Colors

This list includes the basic information about color use in magic, as well as some correspondences for numerology and a bit of folklore. The color of a stone often indicates its type of use in magic.

Red has always been associated with passion, probably because our blood is red. It has also been used to denote royalty, power, and leadership and has been used to symbolize war and vengeance. Red has been linked to the number 9 in numerology, and is associated with the god Mars. The rays of the color red are heat-giving, so it's no wonder red, a "warm" color, has these meanings assigned to it. Other traits associated with red are: physical energy, stamina, sexuality, activity, survival, and passion.

Orange is a color that can be used to dissolve blockages and barriers to a goal—it is essentially red tempered with yellow and is often an effective healing color because it contains the strength of red with the softness of the sunny shade of yellow. Characteristics of orange are: vitality, ambition, fertility, creativity, and stress reduction. No numerical association.

Yellow and gold have long been associated with the sun and the positive attributes of its life-giving rays. Other key words: optimism, success, satisfaction, generosity, organization, and order. No numerical association.

Green has often been thought to be the most pleasing color to the eye—the lush green of forests and plants symbolizes fertility and green is often considered to represent hope, happiness, and change. Associated with the number 5 and the god Mercury (and some sources say the goddess Venus as well). Green is often used to represent nature and, because this color is lovely to look at, it was believed to cure ailments pertaining to eyesight. Also characteristic of friendship, freedom, harmony, peace, empathy, renewal, and adaptation.

Blue has long been symbolic of the heavens, due to the color of the sky. It's associated with beauty, the goddess Venus, and the number 6. Blue is also associated with wisdom and spirituality, faithfulness, loyalty, responsibility, respect, understanding, and the smooth flow of communication (due to its relationship with the throat chakra); sometimes used to stimulate inspiration. A soothing, cool, and calming color.

Violet is sometimes linked to justice and judgment, also a color of royalty and industry. It's associated with age and wisdom, the god Jupiter, and the number 3. In addition, shades of purple and violet represent spirituality, insight, transformation, determination, and devotion. Think of this color, especially in its darker shades, containing the qualities of its combination of red and blue. This means purple contains the coolness of blue with the heat and energy of red.

White or colorless stones (and pearls) always seem to be linked to the moon. Sometimes, however, the diamond, due to its radiant sparkle, was associated with the sun. White also represents purity and friendship. In some cultures, white is a mourning color. White is linked to the number 7. White also represents sincerity, clarity, truth, innocence, perfection, and immortality. White contains potential since it's the complete spectrum of all colors. Also often used to represent spirituality.

Black is a color of gravity and wisdom—a somber color, and also a color of mourning in some societies. It is usually associated with Saturn and the number 8. Other characteristics are: elegance, security, detachment, and seclusion. Black and white are true opposites, yet similar in some ways: black contains all colors and absorbs them and so since black, like white, contains all colors, they have this trait in common. Yet black holds all the colors in while white sends them out. Black represents rest and repose, the inward journey, the soul—as opposed to the pure white light of spirit, an uplifting an outward expression. Black and white are most commonly seen together in the yin-yang symbol. Black also represents things hidden, a time of dormancy, and preparation for growth—it's also a good grounding and protective color.

Geometric Shapes

- **square** = order, stability, four directions
- **circle** = continuity, spirituality, connectedness, cycles
- **triangle** = trinity, body-mind-spirit
- **spiral** = growth and movement (our DNA forms in spirals; the DNA spiral is a golden section)

Glossary

Amorphous: Literally, "without form"; applied to rocks and minerals that lack definite crystal structure.

Amulet: Magical item worn or carried for protection or to repel something (such as negativity). See *talisman.*

Archetype: As defined by Carl Jung, types of universal human instincts, impulses, characters, etc., which have become the common idea of myths.

Aromatherapy: The use of essential oils from plants to affect well-being. Scents are inhaled or used in bath or massage.

Aura: Subtle energy field that is said to surround a person or object (see also *subtle bodies*).

Chakra: From Sanskrit, means "wheel"—these are energy centers in the body that each pertain to a state of mind or physical area.

Charge: In magical terms, to mentally project a specific type of energy into an object.

Cleavage: The property of a mineral that allows it to break along a smooth plane surface.

Crystal: A solid material with an orderly atomic arrangement.

Crystal habit: The actual form of a crystal; determined by the shape and relative proportions of the crystal faces.

Crystal symmetry: The repeat pattern of crystal faces, caused by the ordered internal arrangement of a mineral's atoms.

Crystal system: The structure or lattice arrangement of atoms in the internal structure of a crystal.

Dominant hand/projective: In magical practice, the hand you write with, or use most often. Used to project energy.

Element: In magic, refers to the four classical elements of earth, air, fire, and water, without which life as we know it would not be possible—Spirit is sometimes considered to be a fifth element.

Esbat: A ritual, celebration, or meeting often associated with Wiccan practices; usually monthly at the time of a specific moon phase.

Fibonacci Sequence: Pattern discovered in the 12th century by Leonardo Fibonacci. Starting with 0 and 1, each new number in the series is the sum of the two before it. 0, 1, 1, 2, 3, 5, 8, 13, 21, 34, 55, 89, 144…This pattern occurs in nature in many places: the seed heads of flowers, the spiral of pine cones and pineapples, and the way stems and leaves are arranged on plants.

Fossil: The remains of a plant or animal buried in sediment. Fossils are the surviving hard parts of the organism or impression of the organism in the sediment.

Kundalini: From Sanskrit, means "serpent power." Also described as a "fire snake," this is the energy said to reside at the base of the spine that, when awakened, revives the chakras.

Mandala: In Buddhism and Hinduism, a diagram having spiritual and/or ritual significance. *Mandala* is the Sanskrit word for "circle."

Mantra: a sound, syllable, or words that are repeated like a chant or affirmation—intended to be used to achieve transformation, from Eastern religious practices.

Metal: Solid elements (with the exception of mercury, the only liquid metal) with high melting points; good conductors of electricity; most are shiny in appearance.

Metaphysical: The philosophical study of the ultimate causes and underlying nature of things.

Mineral: Naturally forming, usually inorganic, crystalline substances with characteristic physical and chemical properties determined by their composition and internal structure.

Neo-Pagan: "New" Paganism, referring to modern polytheistic religious beliefs, including Wicca and modern Witchcraft.

New Age: A term often used to refer to eclectic beliefs and practices that rose to popularity in the U.S. during the 1960s and 1970s and have evolved into current use—a collection of esoteric and spiritual techniques that blend Eastern and Western philosophies, ancient and modern. Often including astrology, crystal healing, transcendental meditation, aromatherapy, etc.

Ore: A metal-bearing mineral or rock, or a native metal, often mined for profit; a mineral or natural product serving as a source of some nonmetallic substance, as sulfur.

Organic: Pertaining to or derived from life, usually in reference to organisms. Chemically, an organic compound has hydrogen or nitrogen directly linked with carbon.

Polymorph: The same chemical compound that crystallizes in different forms.

Receptive hand: In magical practice, the hand you don't write with, or use less often. Used to receive energy.

Sabbat: Eight sacred times of the year that Wiccans celebrate, based on seasonal changes.

Sachet: A small bag often filled with perfumed powder or other scented material such as dried herbs and flowers.

Scrying: Process of divination that involves gazing into a crystal, water, or other medium to see images or symbols.

Shaman: Often a tribal medicine man; someone who practices spiritual and healing arts, divination, and communication with the spirit world.

Smudging: Ritual cleansing of an object or place using the smoke of burning herbs and/or resins.

Subtle bodies: Pertaining to crystal healing and magic, the energies surrounding the body: etheric, closest to physical; emotional, feelings; mental, thoughts and mental processes; astral, personality; causal, links personality to collective unconscious; soul or celestial is the higher self; and spiritual presents access to universal energy but is still individual.

Talisman: Magical item worn, carried, or created to attract something (i.e., good fortune).

Translucent: Pertaining to a solid or liquid medium through which light will travel but no clear image is formed. Frosted glass is translucent, not transparent.

Transparent: Pertaining to a sold or liquid medium through which light will travel and form a clear image. Window glass is transparent.

Yin and Yang: In Chinese philosophy, Yin is "darkness" and Yang is "light" as seen as cosmic powers that interact to create everything in the universe. Not literally dark and light, but a union of opposites that depend on each other—light and shadow, moist and dry, masculine and feminine. Yin is the feminine and Yang is the masculine.

Bibliography

"A Guide to Salt Varieties." *The Veg Kitchen with Nava Atlas*. http://www
.vegkitchen.com/tips/a-guide-to-salt-varieties/.

"Agate: Mineral Information Page." *Mineralminers.com*. http://www
.mineralminers.com/html/agaminfo.htm.

Amethyst Galleries, Inc. http://www.galleries.com/.

Bishop, A. C., A. R. Woolley, and W.R. Hamilton. *Guide to Minerals,
Rocks and Fossils*. New York: Firefly Books, 2005.

Bruce-Mitford, Miranda. *The Illustrated Book of Signs & Symbols*. New
York: Barnes and Noble Books, 2004.

"Chalcedony." *Minerals.net*. http://www.minerals.net/mineral
/chalcedony.aspx.

Chesterman, Charles W., and Kurt E. Lowe. *National Audubon Society Field Guide to North American Rocks and Minerals.* New York: Knopf, 1979.

"Common Rocks of Virginia." *Virginia Department of Mines, Minerals, and Energy.* http://www.dmme.virginia.gov/dgmr/rocks.shtml

"Crystal Encyclopedia." *Crystal Vaults.* http://www.crystalvaults.com /crystal-encyclopedia/crystal-guide

Crystals, Rocks, and Gems. www.crystalsrocksandgems.com

Cunningham, Scott. *Cunningham's Encyclopedia of Crystal, Gem, & Metal Magic.* St. Paul, MN: Llewellyn Worldwide, 1992.

———. *Cunningham's Encyclopedia of Magical Herbs.* St. Paul, MN: Llewellyn Worldwide, 1985.

Dietrich, R. V., and Brian J. Skinner. *Gems, Granites, and Gravels: Knowing and Using Rocks and Minerals.* Cambridge, UK: Cambridge University Press, 1990.

Dugan, Ellen. *The Witches' Tarot Companion.* Woodbury, MN: Llewellyn Worldwide, 2012.

Eid, Alain. *1000 Photos of Minerals and Fossils.* New York: Barron's Educational Series, 1998.

Elsbeth, Marguerite. *Crystal Medicine.* St. Paul, MN: Llewellyn Worldwide, 2000.

Freeman, Mara. *Kindling the Celtic Spirit: Ancient Traditions to Illumine Your Life Through the Seasons.* San Francisco: Harper Collins, 2000.

"Frequently Asked Questions About Quartz." *Collector's Corner.* http://www.minsocam.org/msa/collectors_corner/faq/faqquartz.htm

Garuda Trading: Fine Dharma Supplies and Himalayan Treasures. http://www.garudashop.com/Lingam_or_Lingham_Stones_s /202.htm

Gillotte, Galen. *Sacred Stones of the Goddess: Using Earth Energies for Magical Living.* St. Paul, MN: Llewellyn Worldwide, 2003.

Grande, Lance, and Allison Augustyn. *Gems and Gemstones: Timeless Natural Beauty of the Mineral World.* Chicago: University of Chicago Press, 2009.

Grant, Ember. "An Introduction to Crystal Grid Magic." *The Portal: The Magazine of Magicka School.* Summer 2014. pgs. 11–15.

_____. "Crystal Magic for Intuition." *The Magician.* Tarot Guild of Australia Conference 2013. pgs. 56–57.

_____. "Full Moons." *2013 Witches' Datebook.* Woodbury, MN: Llewellyn Worldwide, 2012.

_____. *The Book of Crystal Spells.* Woodbury, MN: Llewellyn Worldwide, 2013.

Greer, Mary K. *Tarot for Your Self: A Workbook for Personal Transformation.* North Hollywood, CA: Newcastle Publishing Co., Inc., 1984.

Gubelin, Eduard, and Franz-Xaver Erni. *Gemstones: Symbols of Beauty and Power.* Tucson, AZ: Geoscience Press, 2000.

Guhr, Andreas, and Jörg Nagler. *Crystal Power, Mythology and History: The Mystery, Magic and Healing Properties of Crystals, Stones and Gems.* Great Britain: Earthdancer Books, 2006.

Guiley, Rosemary Ellen. *The Encyclopedia of Witches and Witchcraft.* Second edition. New York: Checkmark Books, 1999.

Healing Crystals. http://www.crystalsrocksandgems.com/Healing
_Crystals/SeptarianNodules.html

"Herkimer Diamonds." *Geology.com.* http://geology.com/articles
/herkimer-diamonds.shtml

Holland, Eileen. *The Wicca Handbook.* York Beach, ME: Samuel
Weiser, Inc., 2000.

"Hopper and Skeletal Crystals." *Herkimer History.* http://www
.herkimerhistory.com/HopperAndSkeletal.html

Illes, Judika. *The Element Encyclopedia of 1000 Spells.* New York:
Barnes & Noble, 2008.

"In-Focus: Unakite." *Rock Collector.* http://www.rockcollector.co.uk
/infocus/unakite.php

Johnsen, Ole. *Minerals of the World.* Princeton, NJ: Princeton
University Press, 1994.

Jones, Wendy, and Barry Jones. *The Magic of Crystals.* New York:
Harper Collins, 1996.

Judith, Anodea. *Chakra Balancing.* Boulder, CO: Sounds True, 2003.

Kendra Crystal Ravenrose. *Magickal Crystal Path.* https://www.
youtube.com/channel/UCYhgcBbQZZtpoLKxpYZ4dcA

Kish, Karen Diane. "Shiva Lingham: A stone of oneness." *Natural
Healing News.* http://www.naturalhealingnews.com/shiva-lingam-
a-stone-of-oneness/#.VKRY7dLF_To

Kunz, George Frederick. *The Curious Lore of Precious Stones.* New York:
Bell Publishing, 1989.

Kurlansky, Mark. *Salt: A World History.* New York: Penguin Books, 2002.

Lilly, Simon. *The Complete Illustrated Guide to Crystal Healing*. New York: Harper Collins, 2002.

Martin, Patricia. "The Magic of Rocks and Stones." *Controverscial.com*. http://www.controverscial.com/Tree%20Agate.htm

Martineau, John, ed. *Quadrivium: The Four Classical Liberal Arts of Number, Geometry, Music, & Cosmology*. New York: Walker and Co., 2010.

Melody. *Love is in the Earth: A Kaleidoscope of Crystals*. Wheat Ridge, CO: Earth-Love Publishing, 1995.

"Mineralogy Database." *Mindat.org*. http://www.mindat.org/

Molyneaux, Brian Leigh. *The Sacred Earth*. London: Duncan Baird Publishers, 1995.

"Narmada River Linghams." *Healing Crystals*. http://www .healingcrystals.com/Lingam_-_Narmada_River_Lingams __India_.html

Peschek-Bohmer, Flora, and Gisela Schreiber. *Healing Crystals and Gemstones*. Old Saybrook, CT: Konecky & Konecky, 2003.

Pollack, Rachel. *The Complete Illustrated Guide to Tarot*. London: Harper Collins, 2001.

"Quartz Crystal Properties and Metaphysical Formations." *Kacha Stones*. http://www.kacha-stones.com/quartz_crystal_properties_4 .htm#Trigonic Record Keeper

Rodway, Howard. *Tarot of the Old Path Instruction Book*. Urania Verlags, AG: Howard Rodway, 1990.

"Salt Library." *The Spice Lab*. http://shop.thespicelab.com/index.php /salt-library.html

Sea Salt Chef. http://www.theinkrag.com/seasaltchef/salt_smoked
_cyprus.html

"Shiva Lingham Stone." *Healing Crystals for You.* http://www.healing
-crystals-for you.com/shiva-lingam.html

Simpson, Liz. *The Book of Crystal Healing.* New York: Sterling
Publishing Co., Inc., 1997.

Sjoestedt, Marie-Louise. *Celtic Gods and Heroes.* Mineola, NY: Dover
Publications, Inc., 2000.

Soulful Crystals. http://www.soulfulcrystals.co.uk/trigonics

The Magic of Crystals. http://themagicofcrystals.com/

"The Man Who Traded 4,000 Siva Linghams." *Hinduism Today.* Aug.
1989. http://www.hinduismtoday.com/modules/smartsection/item
.php?itemid=648

"The Newly Discovered 'Lemurian Sprouts' from Australia." *Ethereal
Energies of Quartz Crystals.* http://sugarcanecreek.blogspot
.com/2010_01_01_archive.html

The Quartz Page http://www.quartzpage.de/gro_text.html

The Rock Shed. http://www.therockshed.com/information.html

The Salt Works Gourmet Salt Guide. http://www.saltworks.us/salt_info
/si_gourmet_reference.asp#.U-jdN-NdXTo

"Tumbled and Polished Stones." *Rocktumbler.com.* http://rocktumbler
.com/gemstones/tumbled-stones.shtml

Westwood, Jennifer, and Jacqueline Simpson. *Country Lore and
Legends.* London: Penguin Books, 2005.

"What is Dalmatian Stone?" *Rocktumbler.com.* http://rocktumbler
.com/blog/what-is-dalmatian-stone-it-is-not-a-jasper/

Whitcomb, Bill. *The Magician's Companion.* St. Paul, MN: Llewellyn
Worldwide, 1993.

Index

agate, 27, 35, 38, 44, 45, 48, 104, 120–128, 130, 151, 161, 169, 186, 208, 211, 213, 214, 216, 218, 219

agate, blue lace, 35, 38, 45, 120, 125

agate, crazy lace, 128

agate, dendritic, 123, 124

agate, Montana, 127, 128

agate, moss, 120, 123, 127, 214

agate, tree, 122, 123

agate, turritella 126

air, element of, 142, 143

alabaster, 96–98, 192

altar, 10, 13, 39–42, 50, 51, 59, 64, 74, 80, 82, 86, 103, 107, 123–125, 149–156, 159, 166, 172, 173, 175, 176, 179, 181

amazonite, 30, 33, 35, 44, 49, 169, 178, 186, 206, 211, 219

amber, 37, 44, 154, 159, 160, 162, 169, 175, 186, 208, 211, 215, 216, 218

amethyst, 25, 35, 38, 45, 63, 72–74, 84, 85, 110, 112, 118, 137–140, 142, 155, 161, 178, 186, 187, 197, 211, 212, 214, 215, 217, 219, 220

amethyst, chevron, 38, 138, 186, 219

amethyst, green, 186, 187

ametrine, 28, 187, 197, 215–217, 219, 220

amorphous, 90, 186, 187, 189, 193, 195, 208, 223

amulet, 90, 160, 161, 223

anyolite, 100, 187, 218

Apache Tear, 32, 34, 44, 151, 171, 180, 187, 195, 211, 212, 220

apatite, 25, 151, 165, 187, 207, 216, 218, 219

apophyllite, 30, 49, 143, 187, 204, 210, 218–220

aquamarine, 33, 36, 45, 49, 161, 178, 182, 187, 207, 211, 212, 214, 216, 218, 219

Aquarius, 61, 186–188, 190–195, 200–202

aragonite, 24, 50, 101, 165, 187, 200, 205

Aries, 186–193, 199

aromatherapy, 99, 223, 225

astral travel, 36, 59, 122, 141, 143–145, 162, 187, 189, 198

astrology, 225

autumn equinox, 169

aventurine, 22, 29, 44, 49, 95, 96, 120, 159, 178, 187, 211–214, 216–219

azurite, 26, 45, 48, 144, 161, 188, 206, 211, 212, 214, 216–219

balancing, 33, 42, 95, 103, 122, 132, 133, 146, 189, 191, 194, 196, 204, 208, 216, 217

banishing, 9, 12, 13, 62

barite, 27, 97, 154, 160, 179, 188, 205, 219

bath salts, 5, 15, 16

Beltane, 159–163, 170

binding, 9

bloodstone, 30, 44, 48, 49, 131, 132, 154, 159, 162, 188, 208, 211–213, 216, 218

bornite, 21, 48, 154, 160, 179, 188, 195, 216, 219

brass, 44, 159, 162, 163, 175, 188, 211, 217, 218

bronzite, 24, 25, 44, 169, 188, 218

calcite, 28, 44, 48, 101, 143, 154, 159, 165, 188, 189, 194, 200, 208, 211, 215–218

calming, 56, 74, 100, 123, 124, 132, 186, 191, 194, 196, 197, 200, 219, 221

Cancer, 186, 188–191, 193, 195, 196, 198–200

candle, 3, 9, 16, 42, 43, 51, 70, 72, 74, 84, 86, 98, 99, 104, 105, 111–114, 150–154, 156, 158, 161, 172, 173

Capricorn, 94, 186, 187, 189–191, 193–195, 198, 199, 201

carnelian, 23, 44, 48, 130, 131, 155, 159, 160, 162, 165, 175, 189, 208, 211, 213, 215, 216, 218

cat's eye, 33

celestite, 23, 33, 36, 45, 162, 182, 189, 205, 211, 212, 214–216, 218, 219

Celts, 4, 152

chakras, 57, 59, 70, 73, 81, 85, 102, 136, 146, 147, 189, 193, 196–198, 200, 202, 225

chakra, brow, 136

chakra, crown, 127, 145, 187, 191

chakra, heart, 133, 144, 189, 195, 199, 201, 202

chakra, root, 197

chakra, sacral, 85, 198

chakra, solar plexus, 122

chakra, third eye, 68, 136, 137, 144

chakra, throat, 125, 143, 221

chalcedony, 1, 119–122, 126, 130–133, 188

channeling, 144

chert, 121

chevron amethyst, 38, 138, 186, 219

chiastolite, 29, 162, 179, 189, 219, 220

chrysocolla, 32, 45, 49, 189, 206, 208, 211, 212, 214, 216

chrysoprase, 132, 133, 189, 211, 214

circle, 2, 16, 40, 41, 107, 110, 111, 118, 120, 149–152, 154, 156, 158, 164, 168, 174, 176, 177, 179, 181, 182, 222, 225

citrine, 27, 44, 48, 73, 96, 118, 155, 159, 162, 165, 175, 187, 190, 197, 211, 213, 216–219

cleavage, 224

copper, 45, 160, 165, 188–190, 196, 203, 211, 212, 216, 219

corundum, 141, 199

courage, 24, 28, 41, 46, 129, 131, 132, 154, 178, 187–190, 193, 201, 212, 219

creativity, 22–24, 28, 37, 41, 45, 64, 85, 95, 97, 99, 100, 116, 128, 130, 131, 143–145, 147, 151, 152, 160, 161, 166, 187–194, 199, 201, 202, 213, 216, 220

creedite, 190, 216, 219

crystal structure, 137, 203, 209, 223

cubic, 10, 14, 137, 142, 143, 190–192, 194, 196, 200, 202–204, 210

cymophane, 33

Dalmatian stone, 104, 190, 216–218

desert rose, 30, 96, 97, 188, 192

diamond, 21, 23, 33, 44, 83, 141, 159, 160, 162, 166, 175, 179, 190, 192, 203, 210, 211, 214–219, 221

diamond, Herkimer, 21, 33, 83, 141, 166, 179, 192, 214, 216–219

divination, 23, 135, 137, 150, 162, 171, 172, 196, 201, 219, 226

dolomite, 29, 190, 208, 216

double-terminated, 60, 83, 86, 111

earth, 3, 10, 14, 15, 44, 46–50, 64, 76, 83, 98, 103, 104, 107, 120, 123, 124, 127, 137, 143, 151, 157, 158, 161, 167, 169, 176, 177, 182, 186, 188–191, 193–196, 198, 199, 202, 203, 210, 213, 217, 218, 224

east, 154

elements, 14, 15, 39, 44, 47, 91, 104, 114, 164, 176, 177, 195, 197, 203, 209, 213, 224, 225

element of air, 46, 188, 194, 196, 201, 214

element of earth, 10, 46, 107, 169, 186, 188–191, 193, 194, 196, 202, 213

element of fire, 12, 46, 85, 141, 160, 186–192, 195–201, 213

element of water, 45, 138, 143, 144, 186–191, 193–196, 199, 200, 213

elixir, 12, 14, 17, 62

emerald, 23, 44, 100, 155, 159, 169, 177, 190, 207, 211, 212, 214, 215, 217

energy, 2, 12, 14, 16, 21, 22, 27, 37, 40, 44, 46, 50, 55–58, 62, 63, 66, 67, 69–75, 78, 79, 81, 84–86, 99–103, 105, 109–116, 118, 122, 124, 130, 131, 133, 136, 137, 140, 142, 153, 154, 156–158, 160, 161, 166, 172–174, 184–202, 208, 211–213, 215, 216, 218, 220, 221, 223–226

equinox, autumn, 169

equinox, spring, 154, 156

fairy cross, 90, 171, 200, 218, 220

Falcon's Eye, 201

feldspar, 93, 104, 191, 199

fertility, 14, 23, 24, 73, 79, 97, 106, 151, 154, 155, 159, 161, 191, 192, 198, 218, 220, 221

Fibonacci Sequence, 224

five, 40, 78, 109, 113, 114, 209

flint, 105, 121, 211

fluorite, 22, 24, 29, 37, 44, 48, 142, 162, 166, 190, 203, 204, 210, 214–219

fluorite, purple, 37, 142, 162, 219

fossil, 191, 224

fuchsite, 35, 44, 165, 191

galena, 44, 169, 191, 211, 216, 217

garnet, 23, 37, 44, 104, 155, 159, 160, 162, 165, 191, 203, 211–213, 215, 218, 219

garnet, grossular, 165, 218

Gemini, 186, 187, 189, 192–195, 199–202

geode, 23, 101, 151, 191

Golden Healer, 82, 114

granite, 30, 44, 50, 93, 169, 171, 191, 199

green, 13, 44, 92, 93, 95, 96, 99, 100, 121, 123, 131, 132, 142, 144, 147, 154, 158, 159, 169, 171, 174, 182, 186–189, 191, 199, 211, 214, 216, 221

green amethyst, 186, 187

grids, 1, 16, 19, 109–111, 113, 114, 117, 118, 196, 203

grounding, 9, 10, 50, 83, 122, 127, 132, 141, 142, 171, 186, 188, 190–193, 195–199, 201–203, 212, 213, 216, 217, 222

gypsum, 23, 30, 49, 96–99, 151, 155, 159, 179, 182, 192, 206, 211, 212, 216, 218

gypsum, satin spar, 99

gypsum, Selenite, 98, 182, 212

hag stones, 105, 106, 108

halite, 4, 10, 14, 203, 210

Happiness, 36, 72, 73, 81–83, 128, 154, 179, 188, 212, 216, 221

Hawk's Eye, 201

healing, 2, 4, 14, 24, 32, 33, 35, 45, 47, 64, 67, 76, 79, 82, 83, 86, 87, 93, 104, 114, 121, 132, 145, 150–152, 156–158, 186–190, 192–196, 198, 201, 202, 211, 212, 217, 218, 220, 225, 226

Helios, 131

heliotrope, 131, 188

hematite, 22, 44, 85, 95, 130, 131, 159, 162, 163, 165, 171, 192, 197, 198, 201, 208, 211–213, 216, 218 hemimorphite, 27, 28, 30, 41, 165, 192, 205

herbs, 7, 11, 15–17, 123, 161, 164, 226

hexagonal, 187, 190, 195, 202, 207, 208

howlite, 22, 155, 166, 192, 206, 216

Iceland spar, 189

igneous rock, 104

Imbolc, 150, 152, 153, 159, 167

Inner Child, 21, 55

intuition, 23, 36, 45, 85, 95, 135–137, 140–143, 146, 148, 162, 191, 194, 196, 199, 207, 212, 215, 218

iolite, 36, 49, 145, 146, 162, 180, 186, 192, 205, 214, 219

iron, 5, 8, 10, 17, 24, 44, 49, 83, 85, 86, 90, 121, 130, 131, 159, 162, 163, 166, 188, 192, 200, 211, 212, 216, 218, 219

isometric, 203

jade, 8, 13, 33, 37, 45, 49, 92, 93, 95, 162, 193, 211, 212, 214, 216, 218, 219

jadeite, 92, 132, 193

jasper, 23, 44, 49, 93, 104, 121, 122, 127–131, 151, 169, 193, 201, 211, 213, 215, 216, 218, 219

jasper, leopard skin, 129

jasper, Picture, 127, 128, 219

jasper, red, 129, 201, 211, 213

jet, 34, 44, 169, 171, 180, 193, 208, 211, 212

Jupiter, 138, 141, 186, 194, 196, 201, 211, 212, 221

kundalini, 70, 103, 225

kunzite, 147, 193, 206, 216, 217, 219

kyanite, 33, 146, 151, 152, 162, 193, 206, 214, 216, 218, 219

Labradorite, 27, 32, 45, 162, 166, 175, 179, 182, 193, 206, 211, 212, 215, 216, 218, 219

lapis lazuli, 23, 37, 45, 143, 162, 194, 203, 211, 212, 214, 216, 218, 219

lepidolite, 31, 32, 45, 49, 84, 85, 151, 179, 194, 197, 211, 212, 218–220

Libra, 79, 85, 91–93, 187–196, 198, 199, 201, 202

lodestone, 29, 45, 49, 155, 166, 194, 211, 212, 216

love, 1, 2, 9, 15, 19, 26, 28, 38, 43, 72, 74, 79, 82, 84, 93, 110, 130, 147, 153, 155, 159, 160, 170, 186, 189, 190, 195, 197–199, 201, 202, 212, 214, 217

Lughnasadh, 165, 166

malachite, 31, 32, 34, 35, 44, 144, 151, 159, 169, 194, 206, 211–213, 216–220

mandala, 225

mantra, 74, 82, 139, 225

marble, 94, 196

Mars, 188, 191, 192, 195, 196, 198, 199, 211, 212, 217, 220

meditation, 19, 28, 29, 35, 39, 40, 42, 45, 46, 50, 54, 55, 61, 62, 64, 66–71, 73, 74, 76, 85, 98, 100, 102, 103, 123, 127–129, 135, 136, 138, 144–147, 171, 180, 182, 186–191, 193, 195–199, 212, 217, 225

Mercury, 188, 194, 211, 212, 221, 225

metal, 225

metaphysical, 39, 44, 53, 57, 90, 185, 209, 225

mica, 30, 44, 95, 179, 180, 191, 194, 206, 211, 212, 219, 220

Midsummer, 160–163

monoclinic, 144, 147, 186, 188–195, 200, 206

moon, 11, 12, 14, 22, 36, 37, 40, 43, 45, 55, 59, 61, 62, 65, 70, 76, 79, 87, 93–95, 97, 98, 107, 112, 135, 136, 138–141, 146, 148, 156–158, 177–182, 187, 193, 195, 199, 200, 202, 211, 212, 221, 224

moonstone, 22, 23, 36, 45, 48, 155, 162, 175, 177, 179, 182, 194, 206, 211–216, 218–220

Neptune, 138, 186, 189, 194, 196, 202, 211

new moon, 98, 146, 178–180, 202

numerology, 40, 106, 109, 118, 203, 220

obsidian, 30, 32, 34, 44, 151, 159, 162, 171, 180, 187, 195, 208, 211, 212, 216–218

obsidian, snowflake, 30, 180, 195, 217

olivine, 44, 169, 196, 211, 214

onyx, 24, 30, 44, 120, 131, 159, 162, 171, 188, 195, 208, 211–213, 216, 219

opal, 23, 38, 44, 90–93, 155, 162, 195, 208, 211, 214, 215, 217, 219 ore, 21, 179, 188, 195, 217, 225

orthorhombic, 145, 187–189, 192, 194, 196, 200–202, 205

Ostara, 74, 154–157

peacock ore, 21, 179, 188, 195

pearl, 21, 45, 162, 175, 182, 195, 208, 211, 212, 214, 215

pentacle, 46, 47

pentagram, 47

peridot, 26, 31, 44, 155, 169, 196, 205, 211, 212, 215–219

petrified wood, 32, 44, 169, 196, 217, 220

pewter, 44, 196, 211, 217–219

Picasso Stone, 23, 29, 49, 94, 95, 196, 216–218

Pisces, 61, 140, 148, 186–191, 193, 195, 198–200, 202

planets, 138

platinum, 45, 196, 203, 211, 216, 220

Plato, 4, 208, 209

Platonic Solids, 136, 137, 208–210

polymorph, 194, 226

prosperity, 13, 23, 115, 159, 187, 188, 190, 191, 194, 196, 199, 201, 212, 217

protection, 8–11, 13, 16, 23–25, 38, 90, 105, 107, 171, 186, 188, 192–194, 196, 199, 201, 202, 211, 212, 218, 223

psychic ability, 23, 59, 135, 138, 144, 146, 161, 162, 186, 188, 218

pyramid, 203, 205, 210

pyrite, 24, 44, 101, 143, 159, 162, 166, 177, 194, 196, 203, 210–212, 216–218

pyrolusite, 44, 196, 216, 217

quarter, 79, 149, 151, 152, 157, 177

quartz, 1, 3, 11, 16, 24, 26, 28, 29, 32–38, 40, 41, 43, 44, 47, 50, 51, 53–65, 67–80, 83–87, 93, 95, 102, 104, 109, 110, 112, 115, 116, 118, 119, 121, 132, 138–141, 144, 146, 152, 154–156, 166, 167, 171, 172, 175, 177, 180, 181, 186, 190–192, 197–199, 201, 202, 208, 211, 213–220

quartz cluster, 56

quartz point, 11, 43, 47, 51, 54, 58, 68, 75, 79, 86, 87, 118, 144, 146, 172

quartz, aqua aura, 37, 80, 197, 216, 217

quartz, Barnacle, 54

quartz, Bridge, 55

quartz, Drusy, 56

quartz, Elestial, 57

quartz, Etched, 54, 58

quartz, Faden, 59

quartz, Fairy, 72–74

quartz, Fenster, 57, 60, 61

quartz, Key, 61

quartz, Laser Wand, 62

quartz, lavender, 36, 38, 54, 84, 140, 197, 216–219

quartz, lithium, 68, 84, 85, 197, 214, 215, 217, 219, 220

quartz, Manifestation, 63

quartz, milky, 35, 73, 110, 139, 180, 186, 197, 218, 219

quartz, Multi-Trigger, 78, 79

quartz, Phantom, 64

quartz, rose, 3, 24, 26, 84, 110, 140, 155, 197, 198, 202, 213, 214, 217, 218, 220

quartz, Scepter, 67

quartz, Sheet, 68

quartz, Shovel, 68, 69

quartz, Singing, 62, 69, 70

quartz, Skeletal, 60, 61

quartz, smoky, 28, 32, 33, 41, 112, 118, 138, 139, 171, 172, 180, 186, 198, 216, 217

quartz, Spiral, 70, 71

quartz, Spirit, 47, 60, 72–75, 177

quartz, Sprouting, 57, 71, 72

quartz, Stacked, 75

quartz, Striated, 58, 76

quartz, tangerine, 44, 85, 86, 156, 198, 213, 216, 218, 219

quartz, Tabby, 76, 77

quartz, Tibetan, 29, 86, 87, 198, 216–219

quartz, Trigger, 77

quartz, Twin, 79

quartz, with rutile, 166, 198

quartz, with tourmaline, 198

quartz, window, 60

rainbow, 60, 82

record keeper, 63, 65, 66

relaxation, 37, 188, 192, 197, 219

reversed record keeper, 65, 66

rhodocrosite, 26, 44, 159, 160, 162, 198, 216–218, 220

rhondonite, 199

rhyolite, 29, 30, 121, 160, 171, 199

ritual, 2, 16, 17, 35, 40, 50, 62, 70,
103, 123, 124, 150, 152, 156,
159, 160, 163, 166, 167, 169,
172, 175, 176, 178, 181, 193,
224–226

Romans, 4, 13, 15

rose, barite, 27, 97, 160, 179,
188, 219

rose, desert, 30, 96, 97, 188, 192

rose, gypsum, 97, 98, 218

ruby, 44, 100, 141, 159, 162, 187,
199, 208, 211, 213, 215

rutile, 166, 198, 199, 204

sabbat, 1, 149, 165, 226

sachet, 15, 226

Sagittarius, 94, 95, 186–190,
192–196, 198–202

salt, lamps, 9

Samhain, 170–173

sapphire, 24, 31, 35, 37, 38, 45, 140,
141, 145, 159, 169, 182, 199,
208, 211, 212, 214, 215, 219

sapphire, black, 31, 140, 199

sapphire, blue, 141

sapphire, star, 35, 37, 199

satin spar, 96, 97, 99, 192

Saturn, 170, 187, 192, 193, 195,
200, 211, 212, 222

Scorpio, 186, 189, 191–196, 198,
199, 201, 202

scrying, 58, 61, 66, 68, 139, 172,
195, 226

seer stone, 139

selenite, 96–98, 182, 192, 206,
211, 212

septarian nodule, 49, 101, 102,
199, 213, 220

serpentine, 29, 92, 171, 200, 206,
211, 212, 217

shaman, 122, 226

Shiva Lingam, 102, 103, 219

silver, 45, 94, 174, 181, 182, 200,
203, 211, 212, 216, 218–220

smudging, 81, 226

snowflake obsidian, 30, 180,
195, 217

soapstone, 21, 31, 42, 99, 100,
179, 200, 220

sodalite, 25, 28, 41, 45, 48, 200, 203,
211, 212, 214, 216, 218, 219

summer solstice, 161

south, 72, 84

spells, 1, 2, 10, 11, 13, 19–22, 39,
44, 47, 53, 73, 79, 85, 109, 122,
128, 149, 152, 201, 203, 217

spiral, 70, 71, 175, 222, 224

spirituality, 28, 87, 110, 161, 162, 189, 195, 199, 212, 215, 219, 221, 222

staurolite, 90, 171, 200, 206, 218, 220

steatite, 31, 99, 200

strength, 24, 25, 27, 28, 41, 42, 46, 72, 85, 86, 90, 94, 95, 102, 111, 112, 114, 150, 157, 161, 166, 175, 186, 192, 196, 198, 201, 202, 212, 219, 220

stress relief, 35, 188, 200

subtle bodies, 223, 226

success, 2, 27, 29, 36, 37, 43, 81–83, 97, 111, 129, 184, 190, 193, 201, 211, 217, 221

sulfur, 27, 44, 151, 159, 161, 162, 175, 200, 205, 211, 216, 220, 225

summer solstice, 161

symbol, 30, 45, 47, 80, 99, 102, 106, 125, 161, 183, 203, 222

talisman, 95, 129, 131, 132, 161, 187, 200, 201, 223, 226

tarot, 1, 19–21, 39, 40, 44, 46, 63, 137, 146

tetragonal, 137, 143, 187, 196, 199, 201, 202, 204, 205, 210

third eye, 68, 79, 81, 84, 103, 125, 136–140, 142–147, 186, 188, 191–193, 197, 202, 214, 219

tiger eye, 22, 24, 28, 41, 44, 49, 115, 120, 159, 162, 201, 211, 213, 216–219

tiger iron, 49

tin, 44, 196, 201, 211, 220

topaz, 31, 34, 37, 44, 49, 155, 159, 161, 162, 169, 171, 175, 177, 179, 201, 205, 211, 213–216, 218, 219

topaz, blue, 214, 216

tourmaline, 29, 34, 44, 45, 169, 171, 198, 201, 208, 211, 213–216, 218, 220

tourmaline, black, 29, 34, 171, 216, 218

tourmaline, watermelon, 214, 216, 220

transformation, 31, 32, 38, 46, 98, 151, 152, 164, 178, 186, 194, 196, 220, 221, 225

transitions, 32, 85, 126, 179, 189, 220

translucent, 97, 119–121, 123, 127, 130–132, 227

transparent, 96, 119, 121, 127, 227

triangle, 63, 112, 118, 222

triclinic, 146, 186, 193, 199, 202, 206, 207

turquoise, 27, 44, 155, 162, 169, 175, 179, 180, 202, 206, 211, 212, 214–216, 218–220

TV rock, 202

ulexite, 202, 214, 216, 219

unakite, 26, 49, 93, 94, 202, 214, 216–218, 220

Uranus, 186, 211

vanadinite, 29, 49, 166, 202, 207, 218

Venus, 135, 143, 144, 188–190, 193, 194, 196, 200, 202, 211, 212, 221

violet, 74, 84, 140, 142, 197, 215, 221

Virgo, 186–196, 199–202

visualization, 2, 12, 19, 38, 56, 78, 124, 135, 137, 144

water, element of, 45, 135, 141

Wicca, 225

winter solstice, 174, 175

wisdom, 22, 23, 31, 36–38, 42, 49, 76, 87, 100, 102, 110, 136, 140, 141, 143, 150, 162, 167, 189, 193–195, 198, 199, 202, 212, 215, 218, 221, 222

witch, 105

wulfenite, 22, 42, 162, 202, 204, 219

yin and yang, 227

Yule, 174

zebra rock, 25, 35, 166, 180, 202, 218, 219

zebra stone, 202, 216

zircon, 21, 44, 159, 162, 202, 204, 210, 211

zoisite, 100, 187, 202, 216